PRAISE FOR
Running Down a Dream

"What I love about this book is that Tim tells the truth. He not only shares his wins as he pursued his dream, but also his devastating failures. Everybody faces challenges when starting something new and this book is the secret sauce in overcoming them."

—Barbara Corcoran, founder of
The Corcoran Group, author, and *Shark Tank* investor

"*Running Down a Dream* is a book about how to do the thing most people want to do but tell themselves is too scary, too hard, too unlikely. Tim Grahl is not some once-in-a-million-years genius. He's an ordinary person who has managed to do what most ordinary people think is impossible. That's why you should listen to him."

—Ryan Holiday, bestselling author
of *Ego Is the Enemy* and *The Obstacle Is the Way*

"I've known Tim for a decade, but I had no idea what a skilled storyteller he was. In *Running Down a Dream*, he shatters the mold of a typical self-help book by offering a fresh perspective—and an array of life-changing advice—on creativity, success, and happiness."

—Daniel H. Pink, bestselling
author of *When* and *Drive*

"Full disclosure: Tim Grahl is my own secret guru for exactly the stuff that *Running Down a Dream* is about. My own book, *The War of Art*, was about the concept of self-sabotage as it afflicts us as writers and artists struggling to be our best professional selves. Tim's book is the workingman's tool belt. His gift is to show us in nuts-and-bolts, no-nonsense terms exactly how to navigate this crazy life and how to actually Get Our Stuff Done. Indispensable!"

—Steven Pressfield, bestselling author
of *The War of Art* and *The Artist's Journey*

"What does it really look like to succeed? Slow, painful, terrified, stumbling, humble, and persistent. Tim's amazingly vulnerable story convinces you you're not alone in your struggle and shows a path through it."

—Derek Sivers, founder of CD Baby,
frequent TED speaker, and bestselling author
of *Anything You Want*

RUNNING DOWN A DREAM

ALSO BY TIM GRAHL

FICTION

The Threshing (2019)

NONFICTION

Your First 1000 Copies:
The Step-by-Step Guide to Marketing Your Book

Book Launch Blueprint:
The Step-by-Step Guide to a Bestselling Launch

RUNNING DOWN A DREAM

YOUR ROAD MAP TO
WINNING CREATIVE BATTLES

TIM GRAHL

BLACK IRISH ENTERTAINMENT LLC

Black Irish Entertainment LLC
223 Egremont Plain Road
Pmb 191
Egremont, MA 01230

First Black Irish Entertainment
Paperback edition July 2018

For information about special
discounts for bulk purchases,
Please visit www.blackirishbooks.com

ISBN: 978-1-936891-55-9
Ebook: 978-1-936891-57-3

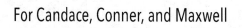
For Candace, Conner, and Maxwell

RUNNING DOWN A DREAM

I'm running down a dream,
That never would come to me
Working on a mystery
Going wherever it leads
Running down a dream

—Tom Petty,
Running Down a Dream

IT'S DARK OUTSIDE.

Late fall. The sun sets earlier and earlier each day. I've always hated this time of year. It's sad. You get up and go to work when it's dark, and it's dark again by the time you get home.

I'm home now, sitting at our small IKEA table I use to pay our bills. I take a deep breath as I stare at the check in my hand. The more I look at it, the more despair settles over me. I toss it on the table next to the open envelope torn across my parents' return address and push myself up. I take the nine steps to join my family in our tiny kitchen in the small house that I can't afford.

Candace is standing at the furthest counter, her back to me, preparing dinner. Conner, our nine-month-old, bops around in his Jumperoo watching his mom work.

I don't say anything.

I just stand there, taking it all in.

LET'S BACK UP SIX MONTHS.

Everything was pretty close to perfect.

I had a day job with great health insurance and paid vacation. I had also built up my side business to a place where it was bringing in enough money to support us.

People around town appreciated my skills too.

My uncle-in-law put my name in at his company, one of the best employers in town. They offered me a job with more money, better benefits and longer vacation. I turned it down because I wouldn't be able to manage my side projects and give my commitment to the corporation at the same time.

And then, two months after our first son Conner was born, Candace and I agreed that I could do the thing I thought everyone else at work was too afraid to do.

I turned in my two-weeks notice.

I would go it alone and build my own thing.

I was so proud of myself.

All my friends were talking about starting their own businesses and pursuing their dreams, but I was the only one with the guts to do it.

NOW I WAS OUT OF MONEY.

It wasn't just "I," either.

We were out of money. We had barely enough in our bank account to pay for food, much less a car payment, mortgage payment, water bill, electric bill, gas bill, and everything else that went into surviving.

I pictured us having to move into my in-laws' house. Every morning I'd have to have coffee with the man whose daughter and grandson I was too much of a failure to provide for.

Desperate, I called my parents and whimpered for help.

Could they send me a check out of the money they'd saved to retire?

I left the kitchen, went upstairs into our one tiny bathroom, closed the door, sat on the toilet, and broke down.

What was wrong with me?

Why couldn't I do this?

Why was I so broken?

It wasn't even that something big had gone wrong.

I didn't lose my biggest client.

There wasn't some big, unexpected bill that came along.

No, this was on me.

Every day I would get up, go into my office, and then waste most of the day playing video games, talking with friends, and avoiding my work.

Then as the day neared its end, I'd panic and start trying to get a bunch of work done, but it would soon be time to go home. The entire drive back to my house I'd feel the shame of wasting another day and make bold, audacious promises to myself that tomorrow would be different.

But then it wasn't.

Stack up enough of those useless days, and you have a bunch of clients that are mad because their work isn't done.

And when you don't do your work, the clients can't be billed. Soon, you don't have any money coming in. Your bank account runs dry. You've put yourself in a place that forces you to call your parents to ask them to send you a check because you're going to miss a mortgage payment if they don't.

Which leads to a truly horrifying realization...*I'm a broken down mess.*

In Steven Pressfield's book *The War of Art*, the artist is anyone taking an idea in her head and bringing it forth into the material world, be it a novel or a sculpture or even a plumbing supply business. He also goes on to define the attacking force that keeps us from delivering on the promise we make to ourselves—Resistance with a capital "R." He says, "[Resistance] is a repelling force. It is negative. Its aim is to shove us away, distract us, prevent us from doing our work."

In one of my motivated states late in the day at my desk, I got around to finally reading Pressfield's book.

In my turmoil on the toilet, I realized that I was Resistance's plaything—stuck and oblivious to its power. And it seemed like the harder I rallied to get a grip on it, the further I slipped into its abyss.

The most devastating line for me in *The War of Art* is the fourth sentence on the last page of the book. In speaking on the artist's life. Pressfield says, "Do it or don't do it."

I thought about that line and the only thought in my head was, "But what if I can't?"

I HAD SO MANY THINGS INSIDE OF ME THAT I WANTED TO LET OUT.

I wanted to write.

I wanted to build a business.

I wanted to speak.

I wanted to teach.

I wanted to use what was inside of me to make this world a better place.

I desperately wanted to "do it," but I just couldn't. I was stuck. And I felt so much shame, resentment, and jealousy when I looked at the world around me.

Every book or article I read seemed to be filled with people making big leaps to pursue their dreams and succeeding.

Why couldn't I do that?

What was wrong with me?

So I stayed alone on the toilet crying and thought it through.

I knew I was broken. There was something about me that just couldn't let me do all these things I wanted to do.

But I had an escape hatch. There was an easy way out of this mess I had created.

I had a degree in Computer Science (also paid for by my parents) and was a pretty good software developer. I could go back to the big company that offered me the big job I had turned down and tell them I'd had a change of heart.

If that didn't work out, I could maybe go back to my old job that wasn't as big of a deal, but honorable and reliable, and see if they would take me back. Either way, I was sure I could find a job that would give me a steady paycheck, a paid vacation, a 401k, and decent health insurance for my growing family.

The tears stopped flowing and my breathing wasn't so labored anymore.

My other option was to double down on my failure and try to figure out how to fix myself.

I could go deeper into this thing and see if there was a way to get myself out of this hole and start achieving some of those dreams I had.

So, I guess Pressfield was right. Only my options were reversed.

He said, "Do it or don't do it."

In this case "don't do it" meant going back and getting my old job.

I realized it wasn't about "can't." I wasn't being physically restrained from making a decision and there was no law that stopped me either. That's a powerful thing to understand.

I had a choice.

I WAS GOING TO DO IT.

I'd face daily Resistance head on and fix my broken self by bringing my ideas into the material world as best as I could. And I knew it would be okay if I didn't do it too. If everything fell apart completely, I'd retreat and regroup. I'd use a valuable skill I had to stockpile some money and buy me time to do it again down the road.

THIS IS WHERE MOST STORIES
ABOUT "SUCCESSFUL" PEOPLE END.

The artist decides "I'm going to do it!" She readies her soul, dons the armor, and sets out to vanquish the dragon. She's on a mission and nothing will stop her.

It wasn't like that for me at all.

EVEN THOUGH I'D DECIDED TO "DO IT," I STILL SAW MYSELF AS BROKEN AND PATHETIC.

Those steps down the stairs to rejoin my family in the kitchen were the first steps of a marathon I was woefully unprepared to run. I wasn't starting on a journey that would be solved over the next days, weeks, months, or even years. I didn't even know I'd begun a marathon.

But I did start.

I was going to run down this dream or collapse in its pursuit. And if I collapsed, I'd get up, rest and then get back out there again.

And boy would I collapse. A lot.

In my future was a personal mental breakdown, a sheriff showing up at my house with a subpoena from the IRS, a marriage that teetered toward divorce, and too many other descents into darkness to count.

But also in my future was becoming one of the most successful marketing professionals in my industry, publishing a book that sold tens of thousands of copies, working with my heroes, speaking in front of thousands of people, and making more money off my creativity than I ever thought possible.

It culminated into a moment when I found myself at a rooftop bar in downtown Portland and realized I had done it. I had caught that dream I had decided to run down so many years before.

FOR BETTER AND FOR WORSE. I WANT TO SHARE WITH YOU MY PURSUIT OF FIXING MYSELF.

This is my story, to the best of my recollection. I'll start at the beginning—full of dreams but stuck and making no progress—and show you how I've reached those dreams.

This isn't going to be a big picture, high-minded, philosophical journey. I know that's not my gift to deliver.

As we'll see, I'm an obsessive, in-the-trenches grinder. I don't have many big ideas, but I can dig in and learn the skills and tools I need to succeed.

So I'm going to make this process very practical.

When you go to the doctor with a broken leg, you're not interested in him talking about the history and philosophy behind the practice of medicine. You want him to fix your leg.

So if you're like me and you feel broken because no matter how much you want to pursue your dreams, you just can't ever seem to get there, this is the book for you.

I've come to believe two simple principles about achieving success in creative pursuits.

1.   Every single problem is fixable.

There is nothing unique about your brokenness. No matter how or why you are broken, there is a way to overcome it.

2.   Success is inevitable if you keep moving.

The only thing that matters is that you keep going. The only way to truly fail at a marathon is to stop taking the next step. Sometimes you're running, sometimes you're walking, and sometimes you're crawling. It doesn't matter. If you're moving forward, you will succeed.

Now, once you reach that success, you'll discover something truly unexpected, but we'll address that later on.

For now, your only job is to commit to going on this journey with me and to keep moving forward. I'm going to ask you to do some hard, uncomfortable, and, occasionally, weird things, but if you do them, you can beat Resistance and achieve your dreams.

Let's get started.

BOOK ONE

FIRST PRINCIPLES
Crawling from the Wreckage

A MAGICAL VICTORY FOR ME WOULD
BE THE ABILITY TO PAY MY BILLS.

TOOL: GO DIRECT

It's all well and good that I made a conscious decision to press forward and pursue my dreams. I postponed a tail-between-my-legs phone call to my former nine-to-five employer.

But the reality of that dark night of the soul bathroom moment still remained.

I had solved none of my problems. The dragon held all of the treasure.

I was still out of money.

But on the plus side, I had a lifeline check from my parents in hand.

I had a couple of options here. I could deposit the check and catch up on some of my bills, but that would only postpone the problem and put me into even more debt.

My other option was to see how fast I could turn things around.

I called my bank to find out how late I could make my mortgage payment and I took a look at my other bills.

I came up with nine days.

Nine days before things got really bad. Nine days to get some money in the bank before credit ratings would go down and creditors would start calling.

Six months ago I had developed a plan and convinced Candace, the smartest and strongest person I know, that I could do this. I blew a lot of that trust, but I had nine days to turn things around.

My plan was to continue to build up my creative projects while doing freelance web development work to pay the bills.

I had let a ton of that work fall behind, which put me into my current predicament. I had no money coming in because I couldn't bill for work I hadn't completed yet.

One solution to my problem would be to simply finish the work I had, bill for it, and then collect the fees and pay my bills. So the next question would be…how long would it take me to do the work I'd been putting off?

Conservatively, I calculated that it would take me far longer than nine days to finish the current work, bill, and book the cash. So that wasn't going to solve my problems today without me having to cash my lifeline check. I set that answer aside knowing that would be Plan B and kept thinking.

How could I possibly pull in cash without having to stay up for nine days in a row and still not make my goal?

How did I get paid anyway?

The way my consulting worked was:

1. Someone would contact me
2. I would talk with them about what services I provided and then I'd send them a proposal for the work.
3. If they agreed to the proposal, they'd sign my contract and send me a down payment so I could begin the work.

So, if I were able to get a bunch of brand new clients in the next nine days, I could stockpile a bunch of down payments directly into my bank account. This would forestall cashing that check from my parents.

I needed to figure out how to get a lot of clients fast. My current runway for making things work measured in days, not weeks or months.

I started coming up with all these elaborate plans. I thought about buying advertising or maybe writing some guest articles on web development websites.

At this time my office was a small closet with no windows at my church. The day after my breakdown, my friend Matt stopped by the church and we started chatting.

Matt is one of those embarrassingly smart guys. My parents paid a university tens of thousands of dollars to teach me computer programming. At the same time, Matt was going to the local bookstore. He would buy a coffee, pull the computer programming books off the shelf, and teach himself the same stuff for free. He wasn't there yet, but in a few years he would found a software company worth millions.

I admitted my situation to Matt and told him about my ideas for getting more work. He blinked a couple of times and then stared at me.

"Those are horrible ideas."

Matt was not known for his finesse.

"Okay, what should I do?" I said.

"What do you need?"

"Clients."

"Right. What's the best way to get clients?"

I thought for a second

"Referrals?" I said, a bit unsure.

"Exactly. Where do you get referrals most often?"

"Past clients."

"There you go. Send an email to every client you've ever done any work for and tell them you're looking to pick up some more work."

"Okay. I can do that."

I went back into my office and wrote out a list of every client I'd done work for over the last few of years. Then I typed up a simple email to each of them. I told them I was looking to pick up some more work and was wondering if they needed anything. If not, could they give me the names of anyone they thought could use my help?

As I thought back through my conversation with Matt, I figured out what he was trying to teach me.

Always find the direct route. Look for the shortest path between A—where you are—and B—where you want to be. I tend to fill my problems with unneeded complexity and junk that just takes up space. Most problems don't need an elaborate solution. Most problems are simple.

Within three days I was flush with new clients. They paid me deposits on the work, and I was able to pay my mortgage and catch up on other bills. I couldn't believe it. It seemed so easy.

I didn't have to deposit that lifeline check from my parents, but my problems weren't over. I'd slapped a temporary cast on a problem that ran far deeper than I imagined.

"WHAT ARE YOU DOING ALL DAY?"

TOOL: TELL YOURSELF THE TRUTH

I was back in the hole again. After turning things around a few months before and getting caught back up on bills, we were coming up short again.

Candace had gone to the grocery store, filled a cart with groceries, and tried to check out. Her debit card came up rejected. Our bank account was overdrawn again. As the checker, bagger, and other people in line watched, Candace picked Conner up out of the cart and carried him to the car, leaving the groceries behind.

"What are you doing all day?" she asked me when she got home.

I gave all the excuses.

I was working hard, but projects weren't getting finished so I couldn't invoice.

I'd been trying to find new work, but it wasn't coming in.

Clients were late paying their bills.

But the truth was, I didn't know what I was doing all day. I would go into the office at eight and be there for nine hours, but somehow I wasn't making enough money.

Sure, I was wasting time here and there. I would play video games a little bit. I'd surf the internet. I'd chat with my buddy Dan, who worked down the hall. But all that was normal.

After this "conversation," though, I got curious. I heard about this software you could install on your computer that would track everything you were doing all day. It tracked what applications you were using, what sites you were visiting, etc. It also categorized everything so you could see what percentage of time you were working and not working.

I installed it on a Monday morning, and when I looked at the report on Friday...I was appalled.

That little bit of time I was playing video games was almost ten hours over the course of the week. That normal web surfing was another fifteen. Chatting with Dan? Well it couldn't track that, but it did track times my computer was idle during work hours and that was another good chunk of time.

I was at work, but I wasn't working.

I realized that my excuse of being too busy wasn't real. Another freaking lie. I wasn't too busy.

Then I started thinking of all the other areas of my life. How much television was I watching? How much time was I wasting reading about working instead of working? What were my frequent coffee breaks to chat with Dan costing me?

I realized that this idea of "too busy" was a big fat lie. Saying I was too busy was offloading the responsibility from me. The truth is, I have a huge amount of autonomy over my life. Almost everything in my life is something I choose to have in my life. Everything from the small things like buying a cup of coffee and avoiding work for an hour to big things like being married and buying a house. These are all choices I have made and continue to make.

If I'm ruthlessly honest, there is almost nothing in my life that I don't have complete control over. Things like my race and some health problems are set. Otherwise, everything else is a choice. I can choose what I eat. I can choose where I live. I can choose what I spend my time on. I could even choose whether or not I want to stay with Candace and Conner.

And yet, every time I make the argument that I'm "too busy," I'm acting as if this is something that happened to me instead of something I've chosen. So I made a change.

From then on, any time the phrase "I'm too busy to…" popped into my head, I changed it to "I've chosen not to prioritize…"

Now, instead of thinking "I'm too busy to write today," I think "I've chosen not to prioritize writing today." Instead of telling a client that I was too busy to get to their project, I told them that I had other things I had to prioritize ahead of them.

The first thing that happened when I started doing this was a complete shock to my psyche. I was devastated by what I saw. Now when I looked back on a day at work when I didn't get anything done, I had to admit that I prioritized so many things above things I said were important to me.

Then the natural next step was to start shaming myself. How could I be so stupid? How could I be so wasteful with my time? There's that Resistance coming forward again. Be forewarned, he's a nasty sucker who will do anything, ANYTHING, to get you to quit your forward movement.

I immediately pushed back from this. I couldn't turn it into a moral life sentence judgment on myself…even if it was accurate at times. At this point it was useless to start labeling things as right and wrong—or a good versus bad way to spend my time. My goal was to pay my bills and take care of my family without having to cash my parents' check or go back to work for someone else. But right now it was just about seeing the truth.

The important thing to remember was that YES! some things were more important than others. I had to focus on what those things were to me without getting all intellectual about it.

When Conner was up all night screaming and crying, helping Candace was a higher priority than getting a full eight hours of sleep. But binge watching my favorite television show probably wasn't.

At this point, though, looking at my situation with open eyes and forcing myself to see the truth about how I was spending my time was the first step. Only after that could I actually do something about it.

SEEING MY TIME-WASTING
DATA WASN'T ENOUGH.

TOOL: STOP DOING EVERYTHING

Admitting to myself how much time I was wasting during the day was enlightening, but not a lot changed. I uninstalled World of Warcraft from my computer so I couldn't play it during office hours, but I burned that time doing something else. My tiny little tweaks weren't enough to break the macro habit.

I needed a shock to the system, something that would force me to change my deeply entrenched behavior. I needed to cut all this useless crap out of my life that was keeping me from doing my work. This would force me to sit down and make progress.

So I got a piece of paper and a pen and I wrote down everything I did in a day. Everything. All the tiny minutia like going to the bathroom, driving to work, and making lunch. I included eating dinner with the family, making client calls, and watching TV before bed. It all went down in one giant list.

Then I went straight down the page and started crossing stuff off.

Here is the criteria/value structure I used to whittle my life down to its core: If I didn't need it to survive or keep my family's life going, it got crossed off.

So using the bathroom didn't get crossed off. Eating dinner with my family, picking up groceries, making a client phone call...that all stayed. But watching TV, reading the news, checking my favorite websites, listening to music in the car, getting coffee with Dan...that all got crossed off.

Then I rewrote the list. I only kept the stuff that was important to the survival of my family.

I lived like that for one week.

For seven days I didn't do anything that wasn't necessary in my life. I didn't read novels. I didn't exercise. I didn't idly surf the internet. I didn't watch television.

This was hard. More than hard, it was excruciating. I ran out of stuff to do at work by noon. I found myself sitting upstairs on the bed by myself at 7:30 p.m. (because Candace was watching TV downstairs) staring at the floor because I had nothing to do.

I did this for seven days.

Somewhere in that week, I snapped. I finally understood how much all this useless stuff was crowding my life. And not just my life, but my mind.

It's no wonder I couldn't concentrate on anything. It's no wonder I couldn't get anything done. I was so jacked up all the time with stuff that didn't help me achieve any of my goals. It all kept me distracted from my primary responsibilities as a husband and father. It was like constantly eating candy and never being hungry for real food.

Now, of course, this is no way to live.

I don't want to live a life where I never go out with friends or on a date with my wife or read a novel. But ever since doing this, I look at all those things differently. Their value has risen.

Over the months that followed this week, I came to realize two things.

The first is that I wasn't taking a radical or ruthless enough approach to change. I was constantly making bargains and pacts and capitulations. I would compromise and cajole. Resistance thrives in that gray zone of valueless non-judgment. It loves instant gratification and rationalizing that I could to it tomorrow.

I was this broken mess of a man, and Resistance loved that about me. It convinced me that it was better to make small, incremental changes instead of burning myself out by making big changes.

Months ago when I was sitting with that check in my hand, trying to figure out if I should give up or keep going, I made a difficult decision to pursue a "dream." The problem was, a decision doesn't actually fix anything. Only our actions do. I had to make change. And I was in a position where slow, incremental change wasn't good enough.

The first lesson I learned during this week of empty time was to be ruthless with myself in my pursuit of my dream. Having pity and compassion for the broken parts of me would only keep me sitting still. I had to move, and move quickly. I had to recognize the lie of that nice voice of Resistance in my head as quickly as I recognized the nasty one.

This reminder way station serves me well to this day.

The second lesson I learned was actually a lesson my dad had been trying to teach me since I was six years old.

WHEN I WAS SIX YEARS OLD, MY DAD GOT HIS DREAM JOB.

TOOL: CUT THE UNESSENTIAL

He moved our family to Georgia so he could take the position. It wasn't a big time corporate job. It wasn't working for his favorite company of all time. It was a Little Debbie snack cake distributorship.

If you've ever walked into a gas station or grocery store in the United States, I'm sure you've seen them on the shelves. My dad is the guy who sells them to the stores and stocks the shelves.

He loves the job because he gets to be his own boss. He makes his own hours, works the way he thinks is best, and is directly rewarded for how hard and smart he works.

Several years after taking this position, a curious thing started happening. Little Debbie managers started flying in from all over the country to spend a day riding around with my dad to watch him work.

You see, my dad had become one of the top five Little Debbie distributors in the United States. And he was the only one in the top fifty who didn't have a full-time or part-time employee.

He did it all by himself.

The managers were flying in from all over the country to see how this one man was able to output so many Little Debbies in so little time.

When he first got the job, they trained him on the "right" way to sell Little Debbies. They taught him where to park the truck, how to pull the orders, how to interact with the store managers, how to stock the shelves, and so on. This system was based on years of training Little Debbie distributors all over the country.

Pretty quickly my dad started seeing some problems in how they did things. Maybe not problems so much, but definitely big inefficiencies. And inefficiencies cost money.

My dad always wanted a job like this. It put the power in his hands for how hard he worked and how much money he made in the process. If you could do something faster, or, better yet, stop doing something and still get the job done, that means you can sell more Little Debbies in less time.

Selling more in less time means my dad made more money every day.

So instead of parking around the side of the building, he parked right out front so he didn't have to walk as far. Instead of showing each individual item to the store managers, he would do inventory in bulk. Instead of taking out all the snack cakes and putting them on the shelf by hand, he would simply take the top off the box and put them on the shelf still in the box. And then, he stopped taking the tops off himself. Instead, he paid a couple of teenagers to do it for him on the weekends.

Each elimination of inefficiency shaved off more and more time. Pretty soon he was servicing four times as many stores in a day than the other Little Debbie distributors across the country.

The higher ups in the company flew in to see it for themselves.

Here's the craziest part of this whole thing, though.

Nothing changed at Little Debbie.

Even now, the way my dad does things has not spread to the other distributors. Most of them still follow the same rules and practices that were taught to them without question.

Constantly trimming away inefficiencies in the way you work is a powerful tool. What's even more powerful is that very few people have the discipline to do it.

I certainly didn't have it.

And until I discovered how incredibly inefficient I was, chances are I would never obtain the knowledge my dad modeled every day.

After that week of cutting all that stuff out of my life, I didn't keep living like a monk. I allowed myself to have some fun things, but many of those things I had cut out of my life I kept out.

For instance, I stopped updating social media sites. And I stopped going to the weekly networking group I had been attending. I cut way back on the TV I was watching and stopped making so many coffee meetings.

Here's what was amazing. Nothing bad happened. Not a single thing. This stuff I had felt a constant compulsion and need to do, once cut out, I realized there was no need for it. It didn't add anything useful to my life.

I have found this to be true for most things I've taken for granted. I had these stories in my head that I needed to do something to prevent bad things from happening. I never stopped to question those things until I saw just how much time I was wasting.

So I started questioning everything. I looked hard at everything I was spending my time on and questioned if it really had to be done. Or if I even wanted to do it. Or if anything bad would actually happen if I stopped.

This is not easy. In fact it took me years to obliterate a deeply ingrained story inside my head.

A few years after my monkitude, I was running a busy consulting firm. (I'll get into how this happened shortly.) I was working with authors to help them market and launch their books and it was going well.

Conner, my oldest son, was five. Candace had decided to homeschool him and I wanted to help. I wanted to start taking off Fridays so I could teach him science (read: blow stuff up in the backyard), but I was afraid. I had employees and clients who needed to talk to me. I had work that needed to be done.

The normal work week is five days, so I needed to work five days.

But did I?

Did I really have to work five days a week? Where did this rule come from? Is this something written in stone somewhere?

So I decided to opt-out. But only as a test. I decided for a month I would take Fridays off. I focused on getting my work done in four days instead of five. And when my clients asked to talk with me on Friday, I said I was busy but could talk Thursday or Monday.

And what happened?

Nothing. Not a single bad thing happened. So I decided to take another month of Fridays off. And so on. And now, I don't even think about working on Friday.

It still amazes me that a single week of cutting stuff out of my life radically changed the way I see the world. I started getting good at keeping all the unessential stuff out of my work life. I cut way back on how much time I was wasting on video games, chatting with friends, and watching TV. It opened up all this space in my workday that had never been there before.

And, honestly, I thought I had won at this point. I thought I had finally fixed that broken part of me that was causing me so much trouble. How naive I was.

NOW THAT I WASN'T WASTING MY TIME ANYMORE, THINGS SEEMED TO GET BETTER.

I stopped running out of money every other month, but another problem started cropping up. Even though I was doing a lot more work during the day, money was still uneven.

I'd still have these stretches where my bank account would be running disastrously low. I decided my problem was I needed help.

If I had someone working with me, I could finish projects faster, which meant I could send final invoices faster. So I convinced a friend of mine, Joseph, who was just like me when I started—married with a newborn—to leave his stable, full-time job and come work for me instead.

Poor bastard.

I thought for sure having an employee would allow me to take on even more paying work and, therefore, make more money.

Reasonable assumption, right?

Instead of helping, though, it intensified my problem. Now I had an entire second family relying on my business skills, which were proving to be very shaky at best. My stress level began to spike in two-week cycles, based on our payroll schedule. Now, if I didn't have enough to run payroll it didn't just affect me, it affected Joseph and his family too. And that's much harder to hide from. Adding new responsibility increases the chance for both new opportunities and bigger obstacles.

I lost count of the number of times I would go to the post office box the day before payroll was due. I put my key in the lock praying that checks had shown up. I would often drive to the post office many times a day to check for mail. My hatred of any junk mail grew exponentially. Every time I saw an envelope in the box my hope would soar for those few seconds. Then I saw it was another offer for a credit card.

More than once I had to tell Joseph that I would be late paying him. Not cool.

This was a problem that the check my mother and father sent me to make my mortgage wasn't going to solve.

One morning, the weight of carrying two families on my shoulders came to a fever pitch.

I had gotten up and gotten ready for work the same as most mornings. Actually, this day was a bit different. Usually, since I didn't have clients in the office and I worked for myself, I just wore a t-shirt and jeans into the office.

But today I was feeling good. I wanted to dress up a bit. So I put on a nice pair of pants and a button up Oxford shirt. I was just about ready to go when my phone notified me that a new email had come in. I checked it to find an email from a client saying that he wouldn't be able to pay their invoice that month.

It was a big invoice.

It was due and I was counting on that money to make the next payroll.

I put the phone down with shaky hands and stood for a moment. My mind churned on what to do next. I riffled through my mind, desperately searching for a contingency plan, but I kept coming up empty.

I sank to my knees and tears welled. My body continued to shake and I folded over into the fetal position. I felt like the pressure in my head was going to pop.

I lay their shaking. I wasn't sure how long. It was like my mind shut down. I waited for a reboot.

I felt like I was constantly pushing and running as hard as I could but nothing was ever good enough. Nothing was working. How in the hell did I move from feeling strong and successful one second into a pit of despair the next?

I lay there awhile until the shaking stopped and I felt like I could get back to my feet. I stumbled to the bathroom and looked in the mirror. Red and purple streaked across my forehead and cheeks where the blood vessels had burst.

This position I found myself in was even worse than when I had to ask my parents for money! What the hell?

Back then I knew what the problem was. I had to crack down. I needed to figure out how to actually work and stop wasting so much time. And through great effort, like "crazy" effort that left me twiddling my thumbs on my bed at 7 p.m. for a week straight, I got my act together and consistently met my responsibilities.

But now I didn't even know what to do next. I felt like I was doing everything I knew to do and it wasn't good enough. I'd "beaten" Resistance. Hadn't I? I was doing my work just like Steven Pressfield said I should do, yet still I was here freaking out in the bathroom.

There's a special kind of desperation and shame that falls on you in these moments. When you know what you're supposed to be doing and you're not doing it, at least there is some control. You know if you can just get yourself moving, you can fix things.

This realization is, believe it or not, more devastating.

I thought I had fixed myself. It took everything I had to root out my problem of wasting so much time. But now I ran into a new way of being broken and I had no idea what it was. It was like being sick, going to the doctors, and they couldn't figure out what it was. That's a different kind of fear than having a diagnosis, even if it's a bad one. It's a complete unknown slap in the face.

As I cleaned myself up the best I could and made my way into the office, I made a decision. I needed to talk to someone who knew things I didn't know. The chances that I was the only person on the planet to confront this sort of cash flow problem were pretty small.

In fact, a few months before this punch to the gut, I had met a guy named Josh Kaufman. He ran a site called The Personal MBA and was a business coach. We had corresponded a bit, but I had never really told him how things were going in my business.

Why? I was embarrassed. Who wants to tell a smart guy that you're stupid?

However, it was time to let that go. My personal humiliation was nothing in the face of Joseph not being able to feed his family because of my pride.

I shot Josh a quick email:

"I'm seriously in need of some regular, ongoing business coaching. I'm trying to make some changes and progress in my business and constantly don't know what I need to do or how to focus my resources. Do you have room in your schedule for me? What is your monthly fee?"

He replied back that his fee was $797 a month.

What?

I stared at that email for long while. I couldn't even make payroll. I didn't have an extra eight hundred dollars lying around every month. But I had this intense feeling that I was slowly circling the drain. Even when money was coming in and I was able to easily make payroll and my other bills, I didn't feel like I was getting ahead. I felt like it was just putting off my inevitable demise.

So I took a deep breath, sent him my credit card information, and scheduled our first call for the next day.

WHEN JOSH CALLED ME,
I HAD TO GO OUTSIDE TO ANSWER.

TOOL: CREATE SYSTEMS FOR THE ESSENTIAL

I shared offices with Joseph and I didn't want him to overhear how bad things were.

Josh asked a lot of questions at first to establish where I was in my business. Then, toward the end of the call, he started asking about my systems in my business. I wasn't sure what he meant.

I explained that I had a small, two-man operation. Systems sounded like bureaucracy to me. It sounded like all the stuff I had to go through for human resources at my old company. Or maybe a car assembly line composed of hundreds of workers, robots, tools and machines. Why would I need systems?

He then explained it to me.

"A system is simply something you do over and over to get predictable results."

"Okay," I said, having no idea what he was talking about.

"It's like your car keys," he said. "Do you have a place you keep your car keys?"

I thought about the little silver metal dish that sat on the table just inside my front door.

"Yeah. I drop my keys in there as soon as I get home."

"Right. Why do you do that?"

"So I can find them in the morning when I'm leaving instead of searching all over my house."

"Exactly. That's something you do over and over—putting your keys in the same place—that gets predictable results. You can find your keys in the morning. Instead of just randomly putting your keys wherever they drop, you created a system so you don't lose them anymore. Anytime you find yourself doing the same thing over and over, you should create a system around it and start doing it the same way every time."

"Okay, that's my keys. But how does that apply to my business?"

"Tim, it applies to everything."

And he was right.

THE BASIC IDEAS JOSH
TAUGHT ME WERE TWO-FOLD.

First, anytime I found myself doing something more than once, I should look for a way to systematize it.

Second, systems simplify things. They reduce unnecessary choices. You do things in predictable ways so you don't have to think about them.

Here's what I slowly started realizing.

Each day I wake up with a certain amount of ability to concentrate and focus. While it can be affected by sleep, diet, and some other factors, I am mostly stuck with what I have.

The scary part is every single time I make a decision or focus on a task, I lose a bit of my ability to do another task later. The problem is my brain can't tell the difference between deciding what to wear this morning, looking for my keys, deciding where to eat lunch, and concentrating on my clients' work.

My life isn't just full of the unessential stuff like television and playing video games. It's also full of essential stuff I have to do, but isn't my true work.

Things like getting dressed, buying groceries, making lunches for my kids, taking those kids to school, paying bills, getting the oil changed in my car, and so on.

That's important stuff, but it's predictable.

I had the same stuff in my business.

Writing proposals, sending in tax forms, hiring employees, training employees, and so. These are all things I have to do. They're essential to my life and my business, but they're not my work. They're not getting me closer to my dream. They're putting on my running shoes, not actually running the race.

Since these are essential items, I can't simply cut them out as I did the earlier stuff. I can't just stop getting dressed before I leave the house. People will throw garbage at me.

Josh taught me that I had to figure out how to start managing this stuff so it didn't suck up all of my focus, concentration, and time during the day. I needed a way first to have this stuff take less time and, second, to have this stuff take less focus and concentration.

This is what Josh was trying to teach me about systems.

Another way of looking at a system is it allows you to make one decision today that removes a lot of future decisions, therefore saving that concentration and focus for something else later on.

I no longer have to think about where my keys are.

I made a decision a long time ago, after losing my keys a million times, to just put my keys in the dish when I get home. That one decision allows me not to make a decision anymore about my keys. This concept extends to all kinds of areas now. I own about a dozen different colors of the exact same t-shirt that I buy from the exact same store. Whenever Candace goes to the store, I ask her to look for any new colors in my size and go ahead and buy them.

I also own exactly two pair of jeans and three pairs of shoes. Every day when I'm getting dressed, I grab a t-shirt from the closet, a pair of jeans, and a pair of shoes that matches. I started dressing this way a couple years ago and now I don't have to make decisions about my clothes.

I get up at the same time every day.

I scheduled myself to work out at the same time every day too, so I don't have to think about it anymore. That makes working out a lot easier.

Each of these little things didn't really matter on its own. It's not like if I suddenly started adding some variety into my wardrobe that my entire ability to focus and concentrate would fall about. But these automatic decisions stack up.

Every time I make a decision that removes future decisions, it frees up my ability to concentrate on something more important. I'm not using my mental energy to decide when I'm going to work out today or when I should get up in the morning. When I'm driving into my office, I'm thinking about my work, not the essential minutia of the day, because I already made all those decisions years ago.

THERE'S ANOTHER SIDE OF SYSTEMS
THAT I STARTED FINDING VERY HELPFUL.

I was terrified of talking to clients on the phone. I hated it and would actively avoid it. I was deep in the imposter syndrome of assuming I didn't really know what I was talking about and at any moment someone was going to finally figure that out.

When I'm communicating via email, I can control it more, but talking on the phone constantly terrified me.

It was causing real problems in my business. If you can't talk on the phone, you can't get people to commit.

I would have a new referral come in on a Friday and the person would ask me to give them a call the following week. On Friday, I promised myself that I would call them first thing Monday. But then on Monday morning I was pretty busy with stuff, so I would just call them back after lunch. Then after lunch I would think, well, they said "next week" and if I call on Monday I might seem too desperate. That same excuse could work on Tuesday. Then by Wednesday I thought, well I still have a couple of days left in the week. I'll call them on Thursday for sure.

I have since come to believe that the true definition of "procrastination" is "assuming I will be less stupid and lazy tomorrow than I am today."

Of course, the week would come to a close, I would never call the referral and then I would feel so ashamed that I never followed up. This would even happen with clients I was already working with. They would ask me to give them a call on Monday and I never would.

Obviously this was a problem.

This was letting money slip away just because I was too afraid to pick up the phone. Yeah, it was silly. Yeah, I felt like an idiot and a loser because I couldn't make a simple phone call, but still.

I had to figure out a way to get past this.

So instead of assuming tomorrow I would be less stupid and lazy, what if I started assuming I would probably make the exact same bad decisions as I did today, but planned for it instead?

I knew that when the time came for me to make the phone call, I wouldn't do it on my own. Was there something I could do to ensure I picked up the phone when the time came?

I started thinking back through the previous months to the phone calls I did actually make. What were different about those calls? Was there some kind of element at play for those phone calls that got me to actually pick up the phone?

I realized that anytime I had scheduled a phone call at a certain day and time, I would make the call. My shame of not following through when I promised to call someone at a certain time trumped my fear and imposter syndrome.

When I shared this with Josh, he, of course, told me to systematize it. From now on, if someone asked me to call them, I would set an exact date and time for when I would call them. I even started using software that would allow people to schedule phone calls on my calendar without me being involved.

This solved the problem.

I still hated making the calls. My goal wasn't to start liking phone calls. It was simply to get myself to make the calls.

I'd still be afraid and insecure. But I would dial the phone and make the call because I knew my discomfort for letting someone down at a specific time was worse than my hatred of the call.

SYSTEMS KICKED ME OVER THE EDGE.

Once I saw the power of systems, not just as tools to save me some time but as things I could actually do to overcome my neurosis and brokenness, I became obsessed. If I could use them to manage my fear and shame as well as the normal stuff in my life, then I wanted to deep dive into all of the ways they could help me.

I started creating a system for my systems. I started grouping everything I had to do into three different groups.

First, for simple tasks—things that have less than five steps to them—I just make a decision and do them the same way every time. My keys go in the same spot every single day. Even if I forget to put them in and find them in my pocket upstairs, I go back downstairs and put them in the silver dish.

The simple task system extends to everything with less than five steps. Every day when I pack my workout bag, I count the five things I need to pack as I put them in the bag.

With these tasks, you get the benefit by simply removing the randomness, and therefore the decision-making, from them. Just make a decision to do things the same way every time so it's no longer a decision.

Second, for more complex tasks—anything over five steps—I would create a checklist.

As a freelancer, one of the things I hated to do the most was create proposals. There was always a bunch of tiny decisions and tiny steps that needed to be done. Inevitably, I'd forget one of them and it would cause me trouble. I'd end up having to email stuff to follow up after I'd already sent the "final" proposal. That's embarrassing and unprofessional.

So I created a checklist.

The next time I had to do a proposal, I opened a text document and wrote down every single step and decision that went into its creation. Sure, it took me a little bit longer that time, but from then on the task took way less time and was done the right way every time.

In fact, one weekly task was taking me over thirty minutes to get done. Now, with my checklist in hand, it takes me less than thirteen minutes. (Yes, I timed it.)

Checklists reduced the need to keep all of those steps and procedures in my head. Second, it ensured that I did it right every time because I didn't forget things. Anytime I caught myself doing a complex task more than once, I stopped and began making a checklist.

MAKING CHECKLISTS A PART OF MY LIFE ALLOWED ME TO CREATE A THIRD CATEGORY OF SYSTEMS.

This third category is made up of complex systems to outsource to a person or software.

The first time I hired an assistant, it was a disaster. I had been complaining to a friend of mine about the time suck required to run my business, and he suggested I hire an assistant. I was still running tight on money each month, but I thought this might free me up to work on outreach and pulling in more clients.

So I hired a part-time assistant.

And then...everything got worse.

Now, instead of her making my life easier, I spent a lot of time trying to teach her how to do things. When I would go to move something off my to-do list and onto hers, I realized I didn't really know how I did things.

I had to stop and try to create a system on the fly that I could hand off to her. Or, I would just give her some vague direction on what I needed, and I would get mad a few days later when it wasn't being done right. That was on me. Not her. We parted amicably after I'd realized I would have to really take the checklist system seriously.

I found that if I didn't create the first and second type of systems, I was imprisoning myself to doing everything manually on my own.

The truth is, I didn't really know what I was doing. I would get tasks done and move projects forward, but I didn't know why or how anything actually got done.

But now that I had weekly calls with Josh, I could run all of this confusion by him and he'd walk me through how to process it.

Inevitably, when I was making my checklists, I would find huge inconsistencies in how I was doing things and lots of errors. But once I had created a solid/working checklist, I had something that not only I could do, but I could hand it off to someone else too.

Once I had developed a checklist for how I process and organize my email, I could easily pass that off to an assistant. And realizing that I didn't need the assistant to be literally in my office waiting for tasks while I paid him, I could begin to hire by task instead of by the hour.

Once I figured that out, I had time to start looking for other ways to get other things off my to-do list.

I found that my "commit to an exact day and time" strategy to get me to make my phone calls was becoming a huge pain. I would email someone with a couple of options. Those options wouldn't work for them...so they would email me back some options. Then we'd finally get something set. Often it would take half a dozen emails just to set an hour-long meeting.

So I found some software that hooked into my existing calendar.

It allowed me to pick blocks of time that I wanted to do phone calls and then I would send a link to a website where people could see open time on my calendar and pick something that worked for them. Once I had created a system around when I liked to take phone calls and how I scheduled them, I was able to offload it to a computer to take care of it for me automatically.

The three-system paradigm freed me up from making future decisions. It helped me do the things I wanted to do but avoided. And it allowed me the opportunity to hire someone else to do complex tasks or to simply subscribe to software to automate a specific task.

My obsession with systems allowed me to get more done in less time. Now I had space in my day so I could get the real work done.

All I had to figure out was what is "real work"?

BOOK TWO

BEYOND SURVIVAL
Chasing the Finish Line

I KEPT FEELING LIKE I WAS STILL MISSING SOMETHING.

At this stage in the marathon, I'd come a long way from that night with my parents' check and crying on the toilet. I started to own my decisions and took steps to cut the useless stuff out of my life that was crowding out my work.

Now my work was about first living up to my responsibilities as a husband, father and then as an employer. I literally had to learn how to consistently pay my bills and make payroll.

I also learned about opting-out of all the myriad of things most people think they have to do because "that's the way it's done" but aren't actually helping them reach their goals.

Then after another meltdown, I invested in an expert. I hired Josh Kaufman, who taught me all about business systems. I fell head first into systems and learned how to reduce the mental and time overhead that comes with all of the essential stuff that is not our real, valuable work.

By this point, I was making some real progress.

My business was starting to stabilize. While money continued to be an issue, it was less so, and I had a good stream of clients coming in that were being properly serviced. I was finding some success, which manifests the moment when your previous clients recommend you to their friends, who become new clients…without your having to ask them to.

Great!

But was that the dream? To build a smaller version of the company that I used to work for myself? To just change hats in the hierarchy from employee to employer?

IT WAS DEFINITELY A START.

TOOL: DECIDE ON YOUR GOAL

And a damn important one too.

But from early on in my life, I had a notion of what it would feel like when I reached my "dream." Even though I'd become an efficient budgeter of time, capable of meeting my responsibilities, I was far from what I thought it would feel like when I hit the road.

I was realizing that running a big business wasn't the dream. The more employees I hired, the more trapped I felt. When I heard stories of people scaling businesses to multiple millions of dollars and dozens or hundreds of employees, my palms would start to sweat.

What did that mean?

A long time ago I heard Derek Sivers, the founder of CD Baby and author of *Anything You Want*, say only three things can drive you. Fortune, Fame, or Freedom. None of them are right or wrong. You can get more than one.

However, only one will drive you.

I knew I wanted freedom. Not freedom to travel. I still don't go many places. Not freedom to work whenever I wanted. I still work set hours during the day.

I simply wanted the freedom to make those decisions myself. I wanted to live a life where nobody could make a claim on my time without my approval.

I was also realizing I wanted to do something more creative. I'm not suggesting that it doesn't require creativity to bring brand new websites into the world while giving proper advice to people who want to have an online presence. I simply wanted to increase my range of creativity...to extend it outside my core competency.

I also wanted to take what I was learning from consulting and start making it available to people who couldn't afford to hire me.

That was a great thing to discover about myself.

Huge.

Something inside of me wanted me to boil down everything I knew how to do and make it available to the largest possible number of people who were interested in what I knew.

Weird right?

Why would I want to do that?

Why would I want to take everything I knew—the things that actually made my business work—and share them with people who couldn't afford to pay me my going rate?

I didn't know the answer to that then. But because it came from some source within, the same one that convinced me to head out into this unknown journey to begin with, I just bought in to it as a good idea. I guess that's what people call trusting the muse.

In order for me to move forward with a project like this, I had to open up some space in my life. Creative work isn't like other to-dos on my list.

I can't churn through it in five minutes. I can't sit down and automatically make it happen. I need both mental space and space in my schedule. I need to have my mind free from distractions so I can think about my work, even when I'm not working on it.

This is where all my bootstrapping to this point helped me. I started having space in my day that I could set aside for these new creative pursuits that were outside of growing a business or working for a client. It gave me some space to try some new things.

I DIDN'T DECIDE IT WAS TIME FOR ME TO MOVE TO ITALY AND LEARN HOW TO PAINT TUSCAN LANDSCAPES.

TOOL: SCHEDULE CREATIVE TIME

I spent years working on other people's websites and helping them build a fan base. It was important work—valuable, necessary, and creative. It was my version of taking an internal gift (my coding stuff and computer science competence) and molding it to serve an ambition to take something inside of my head and turn it into a real thing. I had a real thing now. It was my business.

So what was the result of all of the free space I'd made for myself to consider the next step in running down my dream?

I made the decision that I wanted a following of my own. I was going to do for myself what I'd done for all of my clients.

That doesn't seem like a big leap of creativity, but it was a giant step forward. I, of course, didn't know that at the time, but what I was doing was telling myself that I had something to share—something as important as the people I served.

At the time, though, I just soft-sold it to myself.

Just to try something new, I'd start writing articles about book marketing. I'd just send them out to the handful of people who literally told me they'd want to read them. I had actually wanted to do this for a long time but had decided I was too busy (there are those words again) to do it.

At last, I made a bold decision.

I put a block in my calendar every workday from 9 a.m. to 10 a.m. and labeled it "Writing." I treated it like an appointment. If a client wanted to talk to me then, I would say, "Oh, I have an appointment, but I can call you at 10 a.m."

I was ready.

I had worked hard to get my client load under control. I knew I wanted to start writing some of my marketing advice down. I had the time set aside to do it.

When Monday at 9 a.m. rolled around, guess what happened? I wouldn't write. Same thing for Tuesday, Wednesday, Thursday, and Friday.

At first I convinced myself I was preparing to write. I'd make a lot of notes. I did research. I read articles about writing great articles. I researched the best titles to use for articles.

After a few weeks of this, I had to admit it. I was actively avoiding writing. There was no other explanation for how I could have set aside ten hours for writing and had nothing to show for it.

So I used my bootstrapping skills to fix it.

First, I would start getting ready to write at 8:50 a.m. Right when the clocked clicked over 9:00 a.m., I had to start typing. Problem solved, right?

Not really. I never finished anything. I would get halfway through an article, get frustrated or lose the thread, and either start over or jump to a new topic.

Another couple weeks went by and, though I had actually generated words, I didn't have anything useful. I still hadn't published any articles on my website or sent any out to my subscribers.

Now what?

I BEGAN THINKING ABOUT WHAT WAS HOLDING ME BACK.

This not finishing any articles felt different than the laziness of avoiding my work as a consultant.

That was all about putting the work off and distracting myself. Once I had cut out all of the unessential clutter in my life and began systematizing things, I could get the work done.

But I had done that here too with my ready, set, go typing tactic, yet I still wasn't getting anything done.

I finally had no other alternative than to face the truth.

I was afraid.

THIS KIND OF FEAR IS SO ODD TO ME.

It's one thing to be afraid of getting in a car crash, a rabid dog attacking you or a mugger coming out of a dark alley. All of those things could physically hurt me.

But what was I afraid of here?

There was no physical danger in pursuing my writing. Nobody was going to try to hurt me because they read an article I wrote about book marketing.

And yet, I was terrified.

I was so afraid to put something I wrote out into the world. It's one thing to do the work behind someone else putting her work out there. It is quite different to do it yourself.

But again, why?

What is so scary about sharing your creativity with the world?

Why is this kind of work so different from other types of work?

I've come to see it two different ways.

First, when I am creating something, I am digging into my soul to expose something. These aren't widgets being created on an assembly line somewhere. I am putting a piece of myself on the page and then exposing it to the world. When I code up a website and somebody doesn't like it, I don't feel like somebody isn't liking me. But when someone doesn't like my writ-

ing, it feels like that thing inside my soul is stupid and not worth being exposed.

That's much more personal.

Second, the simple act of creation is doing something that hasn't been done before. It's like there's a camp fire and I am walking to the edge of the darkness and then taking a step from the light. What can I know and see in the darkness? What have I never known or seen?

If you've ever done that—even if you are in the safest campground in North America—you can't help but get a lump in your throat when you venture outside the light of the fire.

That terror never goes away because we don't know what's in the darkness. And our minds are experts at fantasizing about bad things far better than they are fantasizing about good things that will happen.

No matter how long any of us has been creating and writing, our next project involves us walking to the edge of what we've known and seen before and taking another big step into the darkness, into a place we've never been.

ONE OF MY FAVORITE EXPLANATIONS OF THIS PHENOMENON COMES FROM ELIZABETH GILBERT'S FANTASTIC BOOK *BIG MAGIC*.

She's learned over the years that fear and creativity go hand in hand, so she wrote a letter to fear. In this letter she acknowledges that fear feels that it has an important job to do and will come along for the ride on every creative journey.

However, while she allows a seat for fear in the car, in the back, it is not allowed to do anything—suggest detours, look at the maps, or even touch the radio.

And, more than anything, fear is not allowed to drive!

It feels really good to make speeches and write powerful letters to fear. I get pumped when I do this.

I feel good. So I sit down and start typing.

I TOLD FEAR TO STICK TO THE BACKSEAT, BUT AS SOON AS I PULLED ONTO THE HIGHWAY IT LUNGED FOR THE WHEEL.

Fear, one of Resistance's most effective emissaries, had me in its clutches. It had broken me down and forced me to waste weeks of writing time.

I'm obviously no Elizabeth Gilbert.

How was I going to fix this?

Once again, I hit a new pit of despair.

I had done all of this work to fix my procrastination and laziness. I freed up all of this time that I could work on something that was mine, not a client's.

But when I showed up for the first time to do this, I met a brand new broken part of myself that would keep me from my creative work. No matter the best damn advice about creative fear I'd ever read.

RAMIT SETHI WAS THE FIRST AUTHOR
I EVER WORKED WITH.

About a year before he published his book *I Will Teach You to Be Rich*, he hired me to help him out with a few things. I did the nuts and bolts work on his website as he built up the marketing for his launch.

As we approached the launch date, I wasn't expecting much. In my mind, he was this kid in his early twenties launching a personal finance book. What kind of credentials does someone in his twenties have when it comes to finance?

He didn't have a big name publicist. There was no money for ads in the papers. He wasn't doing a thirty-city book tour. He didn't do any of the things the big publishers did. Or at least what they said they did on the back of the advanced reading copies of their big titles.

And yet, he orchestrated a campaign that had the book debuting on *The New York Times* and *Wall Street Journal* bestseller lists, the two most well-known bestseller lists in the entire book industry. This was an unattainable goal for most authors, and yet he had pulled it off.

Ramit is a marketing genius. No doubt about it.

And a lot of the early stuff I learned about book marketing was from working for Ramit that year leading up to the launch of his book.

Plus Ramit is committed to helping other people reach their goals. (That's part of what makes him so effective as a marketer.) After our client/consultant relationship was over, he continued to support me and offer help as I grew my business. In fact, he referred one of my biggest clients early on.

Once I decided to start my own email list, website, and book about marketing, I noticed that he subscribed to my list. I knew logically he was doing this to support me and help me out along the way.

Instead, it really messed with my head.

Most of those articles I started writing and never finished were because I knew Ramit would read them.

I would get halfway through the article and start thinking about the fact that Ramit would read it. He already knew all this stuff. He'd be bored stiff.

Plus, what if I got something wrong?

I would immediately feel ashamed if he shot me back an email correcting something.

To be clear here, Ramit had never been anything but supportive. All of this was going on in my own head. I kept telling myself that if I didn't somehow wow the person on my list that probably knew more than me about book marketing, it was a waste of time.

MY FEAR OF SOMEONE, WHO KNEW MORE ABOUT MY STUFF THAN I DID, READING MY STUFF SHUT DOWN MY CREATIVITY.

TOOL: CREATE FOR ONE

I couldn't break out of it. For months. Fear that I wasn't good enough or smart enough to be teaching anyone about this subject was too powerful. Keep in mind, I was making all of my money from authors who were paying me to help them with book marketing. Not one of them felt cheated, nor did they consider me anything but honorable and effective.

One particular day was extremely frustrating.

I pulled up the folder on my computer with a dozen half-finished articles. I was determined to finish one of them right then and there.

Instead, I jumped between three different ones, writing for a while, deleting what I wrote, starting over, writing again, and then moving on in frustration.

Finally, still having finished nothing, I had to stop my writing session to get on the phone with Marilee, one of my author clients.

We were overhauling her website so she could market her books and workshops more effectively. She wanted to start producing more content for her website but was having a hard time. I agreed to spitball some thoughts about how she could fix that.

For her, writing was a long, arduous process. Her books took years to painstakingly write. The week prior, we had talked through a new idea. Instead of her trying to write for her website, what if she recorded short audio clips of her teaching a concept and published those instead?

In our call, she told me that she'd given it a try and loved it! She had already published two on her website and was excited about producing some more.

I hung up the phone feeling great. I had really helped Marilee.

Then it clicked.

I was spending all my time trying to write for Ramit, who already knew all this stuff. And the few times I could get him out of my head, I just saw this group of faceless authors, most of whom I imagined already knew more than me.

Here's what clicked.

The truth was that I wasn't writing for Ramit or authors who already knew this stuff. I was writing for authors like Marilee. Ted Williams didn't write a book about hitting to impress Babe Ruth. He wrote it for future hitters just starting out.

I pulled up Marilee's website and went to the about page where I knew there was a picture of her. I downloaded the picture and printed it out. Then I took my scissors, cut out the picture of her, and taped it to my computer monitor.

The next morning when it hit 9 a.m. and it was time to write, I opened up a new document, looked at that picture of Marilee, and then typed at the top of the page, "Dear Marilee." I spent the next hour writing a thousand-word letter to her explaining a specific topic about book marketing.

It was the first time I was able to complete an entire thought from start to finish without getting frustrated and abandoning it. I read through it a couple of times to correct any glaring mistakes and then removed the "Dear Marilee" from the top, published it on my website, and sent it out to the couple hundred people on my email list.

Focusing on helping just one person helped me break through my fear of putting work out into the world. I realized if I was waiting until I created something that would help everyone, I would never be able to do it.

Instead, I just wanted to help one person.

Then, of course, just a few minutes after sending out the email, I got a response from Ramit.

"Great article! Loved this!"

A WEIRD THING STARTED HAPPENING AS I PUT MY WORK OUT INTO THE WORLD.

People started seeing it and responding to it. Of course, there weren't Star Wars sized legions of fans commenting. But it didn't take much for me to understand that what I had to offer was valuable.

But there was a dark side too.

In working with my author clients, I kept running into a phenomenon I didn't quite understand. They desperately wanted to be the writer who sold tens or hundreds of thousands of copies of their book. And yet, the idea of any one person reading and responding to their book was terrifying.

I didn't understand this until I started putting my own writing out into the world. The mental focus and inner drive it took for me just to publish something was so strong and almost required me to ignore the fact that people were actually going to read and respond to it.

So when they did, I was shocked.

Most of the feedback was good. I found that most people will either say nice things to you or just ignore you and move on to the next thing. They don't feel the need to "set you straight."

And yet, some do.

In fact, one day I received two emails within five minutes of each other. The first said:

"Tim, your posts are like Bible epistles to me!"

The second said:

"Stop it. What nonsense …??? Stop sending me such stupid emails to me."

I had one person comparing my writing to scripture and the next telling me what I was writing was nonsense. Even with the obvious lack of basic grammatical understanding, it still hurt.

Emails weren't the only criticism I'd exposed myself to. I had people leave comments on my website, which anyone could read, and even publish things on other websites criticizing me.

At first, I made the mistake of trying to engage with the disgruntled readers of my work. I tried responding respectfully and logically. I would also respond out of anger and launch a counterattack.

None of it made much of a difference.

EVEN NOW, THINKING BACK TO THOSE TIMES MAKES ME REALLY ANGRY.

TOOL: SEEK OUT REJECTION

I was just beginning. Just starting to put my work out into the world after months of struggling to finish something… anything.

I was willing to publish and then just as I started, a handful of people were ready to pounce and try to beat me back into the darkness.

It was like waiting for a baby to take her first couple of steps and then immediately pushing her over.

Who does that?

I started looking around online for advice on how to deal with criticism and found plenty. I found a lot of great stuff that helped me keep moving forward and writing. Things like, "Focus on the people who get it, not the people who don't" and, "If you try to get everyone to like you, all you'll produce is mediocre work" and, "Anybody who has ever accomplished anything great has had haters."

It's stuff we all know and have seen a thousand times. And it's helpful especially when you're first dealing with criticism of your creativity and work.

However, something I didn't realize at the time was also in play.

A few years into my online posting, I saw a guy named Jia Jiang speak at a conference.

When Jia was a small kid in school, his teacher decided to play a game where the other students would say something they liked about each of the students. When it came time for Jia's turn, he was met with silence. Nobody had anything good to say about him.

That rejection stuck with him all through his childhood and into adulthood. It stuck with him so much that whenever he faced the risk of rejection, he would go the other way.

Jia had a dream of starting a successful business, but he couldn't ever get anything going because he was so afraid of the rejection that would inevitably come. Eventually he came across Jason Comely's Rejection Therapy Game. The game has just one rule: For thirty days you have to be rejected by someone at least once every single day. Jia decided to give it a try. He also decided to record each rejection and post it online.

The first thing he did was ask to borrow $100 from a stranger. When you watch the video, you can see that Jia is genuinely surprised that it wasn't that big of a deal when the person simply said "no."

From there he went on for a hundred days, asking to do things like be a greeter at a coffee shop, give a lecture to college students, and play soccer in someone's backyard.

Through this process, he learned a lot about empathy and how to ask for things, but the biggest lesson was that rejection is not something you have to be afraid of. It's one of those things that our brains tell us to avoid at all costs, but, really, it's no big deal.

I realized listening to Jia talk that I had been doing this in those early days of publishing my work.

And let me tell you, it's a lot easier as a writer to work through the criticism of a five-hundred-word article than it is on a book that took you two years to write. By releasing my work in small batches to a very small audience, I was inoculating myself against the criticism that would come when I released bigger, bolder projects.

If you practice getting rejected, the pain you experience with each subsequent rejection lessens.

SO WHAT CRITICISM SHOULD YOU LISTEN TO?

TOOL: ACCEPT THE RIGHT KIND OF CRITICISM

With the help from Jia Jiang's story, I began to pay less and less attention to criticism that came from strangers or anonymous people. There was no way to know if these people had any kind of credentials or background that would give them true insight into my work. They didn't know me, and I didn't know them. How could they possibly know what was good for me and my goals?

This allowed me to focus on the handful of people I could trust to give me true feedback on my work.

I really took hold of this idea when it came time to publish my first book, which I'll get to in a few pages. In this early time, I trusted a few handfuls of friends, who I knew were paying attention to my writing and would give me real feedback. If they criticized my work, it didn't feel good, but I could trust it was coming from a good place and I would listen and adjust accordingly.

I learned pretty quickly that most criticism is useless and is much more about the person doing the criticizing than it is about the work or me.

Besides, I was dealing with a critic that was so much more vindictive and hateful than anyone could ever be online.

AS I CONTINUED TO MAKE WRITING A PART OF MY LIFE, FEAR KEPT ATTACKING ME IN FRESH FORMS.

TOOL: OTHER TACTICS TO OVERCOME FEAR

The thing that still consistently surprises me is how many different guises fear comes in and the variety of tactics it employs to keep me from my creative work.

I quickly found that worrying about what Ramit or random critics thought of me was just the beginning of the battles I would have to fight to produce anything. Not just good stuff. Anything.

I started writing and publishing more consistently, but it was still an ongoing struggle. Some days it would come out easily. Other days I would get stuck and fight and struggle with nothing to show for it. Fighting fear was like trying to outflank an amorphous blob in the dark. Every time I thought I had a handle on things, it would shape shift again, and I found myself broken down again.

Worrying that other people would think I was an idiot was just one fraction of the thoughts my mind could come up with to keep me off track.

I started developing some other techniques to buy me enough time to finish stuff.

For instance, I promised myself I would keep it a secret.

I would write the whole thing, and if it wasn't good enough, I would delete it and never show it to anyone. That worked for a while.

I also started cursing a lot in my first drafts. If I was going to delete it if it didn't work, why not?

I found if I put lots of "fucks" and "shits" in my writing, I would say what I really wanted to say. Because I was breaking the taboo of cursing, it allowed me to overcome other things I was afraid of saying. If I thought the message was strong, I would just edit out the cursing in the second draft.

These techniques would work sometimes, but other times they wouldn't. Often, they would work for a while, but then the fear just shape shifted again and I found myself stuck.

Nothing seemed to keep it at bay long enough that I could stay consistent.

This would breed other types of shame.

I would tell my clients they needed to be writing consistently for their own websites, but then weeks would go by without me publishing anything new on my own website. Then after those weeks of not writing, I would put all this pressure on myself to write something amazing, which just blocked me up all over again.

I COULDN'T FIGURE OUT WHAT WAS CONSTANTLY HOLDING ME BACK.

TOOL: DAILY AFFIRMATIONS

Around this time, I had downloaded some recordings of live workshops that Zig Ziglar had done. Zig had gotten his start by teaching and writing on the topic of sales. Then as his success grew, he moved into general business and self-help topics.

I loved listening to him and eventually introduced Candace to him. Before long we were listening to him in the car anytime we had a long drive to make.

One of the things he suggested doing was a daily affirmation.

He had written this long page of "I am" statements that were meant to be motivational. Things like "I have character, and I am knowledgeable," "I am disciplined, motivated, and focused," and "I am intelligent, competent, persistent and creative."

Zig's prescription was to stand in front of the mirror twice a day, morning and evening, for thirty days and "stand up straight, square your shoulders, look yourself in the eye and quietly, firmly" repeat all of the statements.

I found the whole thing to be pretty cheesy.

The first time Candace listened with me, she suggested we give it a try, but I rolled my eyes and blew it off. Fast forward a few months and we were listening to it in the car again after a particularly frustrating week of writing for me. I didn't say anything, but once we got home I went online, searched for a copy of the affirmation, and printed it off.

The next morning as I was getting ready for work, I waited for Candace to go downstairs and then I grabbed the printout, went in the bathroom, and locked the door. I stood in front of the mirror, looked at the paper to get the first line, and then looked back up at myself and said, "I, Tim Grahl, am a person of integrity, with a good attitude and—"

My voice broke. Tears came into my eyes. Everything in me fought the words that were coming out of my mouth.

How could I call myself a person of integrity? I told that client last week I would work on their project and I hadn't gotten to it yet. How could I say I had a good attitude? All I had done the day before was complain about how I couldn't get my writing done.

I pushed forward.

I hit the part about being knowledgeable and broke off again.

How could I say that when I knew for a fact that I was an idiot with nothing useful to say?

I scanned down through the page some more.

Hard working? Yeah right. Everyone knew that wasn't true.

Disciplined? Hardly!

Responsible and dependable? Intelligent? Confident?

All things that may be true about other people, but were absolutely not true about me.

I dropped the printout and leaned heavily on the counter. Tears streamed down my face, but realization was starting to come to me.

I HATED MYSELF.

I couldn't say anything out loud that was good about myself without feeling like liar. I walked around all day every day with these thoughts about myself. No wonder I could barely bring myself to do anything creative. I believed anything I created would, by definition, be worthless because it was coming from a worthless source.

I stood back up, grabbed the piece of paper and clutched it in front of me. I looked myself in the eye again and began reading. I fought through the tears and cracking voice and finished every single line of the affirmation. Then I folded it in half and put it in my nightstand drawer.

That night, I pulled it out before bed, went back into the bathroom, locked the door again, and fought my way back through the affirmation.

Somewhere around day seven or eight, I started being able to go through the whole affirmation without breaking down.

Somewhere around day fifteen, it started feeling natural.

By day twenty-five I stopped feeling like a liar.

After the thirty days were up and I finished doing the affirmation that evening, I realized I was starting to believe some of these things about myself.

Instead of pointing out all the ways I was undisciplined, my mind started bringing up times that I was disciplined. I remembered the afternoon I worked hard all afternoon and finished a project on time for a client. I thought about the conversation with a client where I suggested a really good solution to one of her problems.

The awful thoughts about myself started losing their grip over me. My default position about myself started shifting. I also started coming up with my own affirmations.

I realized I was also having some pretty negative feelings about my writing. I would catch thoughts like "You're never going to be good at this" and, "This is a complete waste of time" coming through my head. So I took that worn out affirmation, flipped it over and wrote down, "I give grace to myself and accept that perfection is not the goal, only truth" and, "I am proud of being a writer and consider it an honor to serve the world in this way."

I started trying to pay attention to my thoughts as they came in. If I saw a particularly negative thought making repeat appearances, I would write down the thought and then come up with an affirmation to directly combat it.

I was amazed at the change that started happening. It stopped being such a fight to write and publish my articles. I found that the affirmations were building up a strong scaffolding around the broken parts of me. They kept me from falling apart long enough so I could get something out that I was proud of.

The fear was still there, but it was like the volume had been turned down.

WHEN I WAS EIGHT YEARS OLD, MY
PARENTS AND I MOVED INTO A NEW HOUSE.

For a kid like me it was a dream home. There were giant, climbable trees, woods in the backyard complete with a tree house, and a creek running through the large front yard.

I spent hours in that creek doing just about anything an eight-year-old boy could possibly come up with. I built dams, I dug for crawfish, and I would dig out large portions of the creek to make little pool areas.

I remember that digging out the creek was the hardest task.

It seemed like every time I pulled out a handful of mud from the bottom, more mud would just flow into its place. There were times I looked at the pile of mud I had dumped on the bank and then looked back at the creek and wondered if it was magically just creating more because I had made basically no progress.

I thought about this a lot as I continued trying to open up my creativity. It seemed like every time I would scoop fear out of my life, more fear from some unending supply would flow into the spot left behind.

As my self-talk was starting to get cleaned up, and I was able to spend time on my creativity without constantly feeling like I wasn't good enough, a new form of fear flowed right into its place.

Fear then moved from the internal to the external.

I started worrying constantly about everything. I worried about money and paying taxes. I worried about my clients being happy. I worried about the big projects I was working on. I worried about my employees leaving. I worried about my kids and Candace. I worried if I was being a good husband and father. I worried about my eating and staying healthy. Hell, I worried about mowing the grass and cleaning up the basement.

Each of these worries started feeling like someone tapping on my head constantly. None of them caused any great distress, but combined it was a constant Woody Woodpecker distraction.

THE FIRST TIME I REALLY NOTICED HOW MUCH TROUBLE WOODPECKER DISTRACTIONS WERE CAUSING ME WAS ON A SOLITUDE RETREAT.

TOOL: CREATE A WORRY LIST

There was a small converted convent in the town I lived in at the time. It was set up so you could come in and spend time in solitude and prayer by staying in the nuns' old quarters.

My pastor encouraged me to take a weekend retreat there to be quiet and alone for a couple days. I was a little nervous about it, but decided to give it a try.

It didn't take long for me to get antsy.

I was so used to constantly having something to do. Whether it was work or family or reading a book before bed, there was always something to fill the time.

If I ever stopped doing my to-do list, it felt like every worry and anxiety came crashing into me. I wanted to spend the weekend in meditation and writing, but I couldn't shake the thousands of little taps on the head my fears were causing.

Pretty quickly I broke down and went out to the main area of the retreat center where I knew my pastor would be. I told him what I was dealing with and he smiled. This was the whole reason he had suggested giving solitude a try, so I could see and face this problem.

"Make a worry list," he said.

"What's a worry list?" I asked.

"Exactly what it sounds like. Make a list of every single thing you're worried about. From the big, truly scary things, to the small, mundane things. Get it all out and onto paper. Then, once it's all out, look at the list and promise yourself that you will take care of everything on that list later, but for now, you have other things to focus on."

"Okay," I said, a little unsure. "What if more stuff just keeps coming up?"

"Just stop, add it to the list, and make yourself the same promise. Then you'll be able to concentrate again."

I nodded my head, stood, and headed back to the tiny room where a nun used to sleep. I sat down at the little wooden desk, pulled out a piece of paper, and started writing. I put it all down.

I got really specific.

I wrote down each of my worries about Candace and the boys.

I wrote down specific things I was worried about with each of my current clients.

I wrote down my worries about my employees and their work.

I wrote down my worries about the lawn mower being broken and my dog's limp and every single little thing that I could think of.

Finally, after filling up an entire sheet of paper front and back, I ran out of things to worry about. I sat back in my chair and looked at the paper.

I turned it over, back and forth, a couple times.

No wonder I couldn't concentrate on anything. My head was so jammed with stuff to worry about that I couldn't hope to keep track of anything else.

A WHILE LATER I WAS TALKING TO JOSH ABOUT THIS, AND HERE'S THE PICTURE HE GAVE ME.

Trying to live in the twenty-first century with our brains is like trying to run the latest computer operating system on a computer built thirty years ago.

Our brains evolved to take worries very seriously because we worried about things like finding enough food to eat and making sure tigers didn't eat us. Every worry was a real and present danger.

Now our lives are filled with small, non-life-threatening worries, but our brains have a hard time separating these from the tiger-is-going-to-eat-me kind of worries. So each of those things I wrote down on the piece of paper was like a flashing "danger" sign constantly blinking in my head.

I had written down over a hundred worries. That's a hundred flashing "danger" signs in my head constantly trying to get my attention. My strategy for fighting all of these worries up until now was to ignore them and push them away.

Trying to "ignore" something is practically impossible.

The problem is, the more I "ignored" these worries, the more my brain tried to get my attention with each one of them. "Something is wrong! Something is dangerous! Pay attention!" it constantly screamed at me.

By taking the time to write them all down, I gave each of those worries a voice. Then, by promising myself that once I was done with my work, I would focus and take care of each of those worries in due time, it allowed my brain to quiet down.

As I sat back in the chair and stared at that list at the old convent, it was the first time in my memory that my mind settled down.

I was shocked. I had become so used to the noise and flashing "danger" signs that I didn't know there was another way to live.

I set the paper to the side and was immediately able to concentrate on what I was working on.

The voices, while not gone, were finally quiet enough that I could concentrate.

Of course, I hadn't actually fixed anything. My lawn mower was still broken, my clients' projects were still not done, and I still had young children I needed to raise. But for the first time, just by creating a worry list and promising myself that I would take care of all of it later, my mind finally quieted down and let me work.

I WAS STARTING TO BEAT BACK FEAR, AND IT FELT GOOD.

I built up a good toolbox of options to use whenever fear started holding me back.

1   I focused on creating for one person.
2. I promised myself to keep it a secret.
3. I wrote affirmations to combat specific fears about my character
4. I always kept my worry list close by.

These worked pretty well for a while.

It was enough to get me to write articles or create a couple of videos. It would allow me to relegate fear to the backseat long enough to actually get a small project done.

But a brand new monster of a problem surfaced when I decided to work on my first large project.

ONE OF THE THINGS I REALIZED EARLY ON ABOUT MYSELF IS THAT I AM A PESSIMIST.

TOOL: THE MAGIC WAND

Not a glass-half-empty sort of pessimist. I'm more of an at-some-point-the-glass-will-get-knocked-over pessimist. I wasn't the friend you called when you wanted to get excited about something. I was the friend your spouse wanted you to call to talk you out of something.

This was especially true when it came to my own dreams and projects.

I had a hard time getting excited about anything because all I could see were the potholes and the probable, eventual failure of whatever I was trying to work on.

At this time in my life I was doing a lot of mountain biking, so my buddy Mike and I met up for a ride. We had ridden together for years and had the war stories and scars to back it up. This particular day was perfect for a ride. It was cold and crisp outside. One of those days where you started out cold, but once you got going, you got a good sweat on.

We decided to head up to the Candlers Mountain trail network. It was just on the edge of town and the local college's mountain biking team cut a bunch of new trails that were a lot of fun.

We met at the trail head, pulled the bikes out of the cars, put on our helmets, gloves and other gear, and started out for the ride. We were riding for a while. It was a familiar trail with some good climbs and fast descents.

Then we came to the dam.

This wasn't a big river with a giant structure blocking the water. This was a small creek, mostly dried out, with a concrete wall running through it about six inches wide. At its tallest point you were only about five feet above the ground.

Neither Mike nor I ever had the courage to ride across this dam, but today was going to be different. I'd read an article in one of the mountain biking magazines I subscribed to about how to ride over obstacles like this, and I was ready to give it a try. Mike agreed he'd do it too.

I went first.

As my front wheel started across the dam, like the article told me to do, I lifted my eyes up and locked them on the other side of the creek. Everything in me wanted to look down at my front wheel and make sure it was in the right place, but I fought the urge and continued looking ahead while I pedaled.

I made it across safely and immediately turned back to watch Mike.

He had already started riding across but was in trouble. His eyes were locked on his front wheel and he was teetering wildly. I opened my mouth to yell at him to look up, but it was too late.

With a holler he toppled over the dam ledge.

I jumped off my bike and ran back across the dam to find him lying in a bed of leaves. He was extremely pale and staring down at his foot, which I noticed was pointing off at a weird angle.

An hour or so later after frantic emergency calls and anxious waiting, I helped several fire and policemen carry Mike out of the woods on an orange sled.

His ankle was severely broken.

I THOUGHT ABOUT MIKE A FEW MONTHS LATER
WHEN I WAS ON THE PHONE WITH GENE KIM.

I was working with Gene as he finished up his book *The Phoenix Project*. We were having one of our weekly calls and he was throwing out all kinds of ideas to get the book ready for the launch.

I kept dragging his big ideas back down to earth with my logical pessimism.

Finally, he got frustrated with me and said, "Okay, Tim, if I could wave a magic wand and get everything I want, here's what it would look like."

For the next couple of minutes, he described the perfect scenario.

If everything fell into place perfectly.

If everybody did exactly what they were supposed to do.

If all of the systems worked with no bugs.

Then, he said the words that changed my life.

"How close can we get to that?"

What Gene believed was that if you shoot as high as possible, you may not hit the target, but you'll get much closer to it than you would being obsessed with the micro goals.

My bike trip with Mike proved that Gene was absolutely right. Because I was looking into the far distance on the ultimate goal—getting across the entire dam ledge—I was able to actually overcome all the little distractions and reach the far side. Too often the fear of failing pulls our eyes down and we get so caught up in the myriad of things that could go wrong that we lose our balance.

In my consulting, I was so used to cutting ideas off at the knees before they even got started that I never thought to consider what would happen if everything went right… what it would be like to focus on realizing the big goal instead of worrying about the little bugs that would come up as I was moving toward it.

I realized too that I was always even harder on myself with my own projects than I was with clients. I'd "humor" them and try out one of their ideas. Lo and behold a lot of them pushed us closer to our goal even when they were buggy.

Now I had a big, new project I wanted to start. Could I think big without getting lost in the details?

I WANTED TO WRITE A BOOK.

After several years of writing short pieces about book marketing stuff, I wanted to put it all together into a book.

But I hadn't made much progress on it. I kept thinking of all the reasons it wasn't going to work out. I kept focusing on all of the things that would probably go wrong.

However, after getting off the phone with Gene that day, I wondered if I should use his magic wand for my own book. So I sat down with a piece of paper and, at the top, wrote:

"What would happen if everything went right with my book?"

I started writing out all the good things it would do for my business. I wrote about what it would feel like to publish a book. I wrote about all the people I would be able to help. I wrote about the extra money a book would bring in along with the opportunities I knew being a published author created.

For just a few minutes, I took that pessimistic character inside of me and duct taped his mouth shut. I spent the time dreaming big.

I realized these were my goals.

This is what I wanted to accomplish. This was what I needed to keep my eyes on as I navigated the treacherous territory of writing and publishing a book. This was hard to do, though, because I had no idea what I was signing on for when I decided to write a book.

THE TIME WAS NOW.

I had built up my book marketing consultant firm and it was doing pretty well. There were still lean months, but for the most part, I was keeping my head above water.

There was really no reason to take on a large writing project like writing a book.

The articles I was writing were helping out more and more authors, and they were even bringing in some new clients. I was busy with those writing projects and client work, so I didn't need the hassle of adding something else to my plate.

Yet, somehow I knew it was time to write a book. There's that muse again.

But because I'm a super practical person who can't really wrap his head around things that I have zero control over, I reasoned out why it was time to write the book to make me feel more secure in the decision.

There were a few reasons for writing a book.

First, I wanted to put everything I knew about book marketing into a form that would be easy for writers to "get." I thought it would be a helpful thing for the world. It would teach writers that "marketing" wasn't some magical thing that fairies at book publishing companies knew but they, as authors, never would. It's not that at all. That was the altruistic part of me. And it was real.

However, I am a bundle of competing and incongruent motivations.

I also knew having a book that clearly told writers what they needed to do to increase the chances of people discovering their work would be a good marketing tool for my company. I wanted people to see me as an expert. I wanted the recognition that I was an important person in my field and should be taken seriously.

I also wanted to feel more like a "real" writer.

I kept working with all of these serious writers that were publishing books and, even though I was spending a lot of time writing, I still didn't consider myself a writer writer. You know?

To be a "real" writer, I needed to publish a book. And not just any book. Since I was publishing a book about book marketing, it had to be a successful book.

If I could write and publish a successful book about book marketing, it would finally make me feel like a success in my field and would allow people to see me as a writer, not just a consultant who works with writers.

You see how Steven Pressfield's conception of Resistance is starting to build a wall around this "book" idea?

Something very pure and good (helping other people) starts to get loaded with a whole bunch of stuff that's really all about "me."

And that's good too, don't get me wrong. Because writing a book is very much about "me" too. If it weren't, there'd be no value/creative force inside the project.

But when you start moving forward with the notion that you'll create value for other people inside something you make…this is when Resistance really pays attention. Because it doesn't like that.

WHEN I STARTED THE PROJECT, I THOUGHT IT WOULD BE PRETTY STRAIGHTFORWARD.

I talked about book marketing every single day. I spent hundreds of hours on the phone with clients teaching book marketing. I'd also written thousands upon thousands of words in various articles on the subject.

Stringing all of that together into a book should be easy.

Of course, Resistance loves this type of thinking.

Why?

Because if Resistance can sucker punch you on your first big creative project—something you know you can do with your hands tied behind your back—it knows it will keep you from trying anything else. If Resistance knocks you out in the first ten seconds of round one...there's no way you'll ever get back in the ring again.

I WAS HORRIBLY WRONG. I WAS COMPLETELY UNPREPARED FOR THE TASK.

Sure, I could talk about this stuff.

I could even string together a thousand words on the subject.

But that's like thinking that because you know how to create a single brick, you'll be able to build a perfectly functioning house.

It didn't take long for the project to start hitting roadblocks. I kept getting stuck and unsure of what to do next, so I would start procrastinating again.

However, my new form of procrastination was very different from my old forms. I wasn't playing video games, watching TV or killing time reading articles about writing. I kept writing. I went back to where I felt safe. I kept writing articles for my own website and email list. I focused on getting articles placed in other websites and publications.

Again, I was surprised by how insidious Resistance-generated fear could be.

It tricked me into doing work I used to be afraid of but wasn't any longer as a way to keep me from stepping over that edge into a new kind of darkness.

Avoidance became a chronic problem.

It went on for months. I would get frustrated with myself and dive back into the manuscript to start working on it again. Then, without me realizing it, two weeks would pass without me working on it.

I had this dream of what it would be like to finish and publish the book, but it was too vague and too far off in the future to really drive me to change. The immediate frustration and fear was far too strong.

AROUND THIS TIME, I CAME ACROSS AN EPISODE OF THE RADIO SHOW RADIOLAB TITLED YOU V. YOU.

TOOL: MAKE FAILURE EXTREMELY PAINFUL

It told the story of Zelda and Mary, two lifelong best friends. Both were social workers and had committed to fight racial inequality, and both fought for years to quit smoking.

Mary finally quit smoking, but Zelda just couldn't break the habit. She tried everything. All the self-talk and remedies she could find weren't enough. She just kept on smoking.

After decades of frustration, she did something remarkable to motivate herself. Zelda made a promise to Mary that if she ever smoked again she would give $5,000 to the Ku Klux Klan, the force that stood for everything she was opposed to.

That was it.

After that deal with Mary, Zelda never smoked again.

In order change her behavior into one that had long-term benefits, she had to create a very short-term pain that was big and scary enough to overcome her immediate desires.

Zelda's story clicked for me.

In order for me to force myself to finish this first draft of the book, I had to come up with something extremely painful to avoid.

I knew just the thing.

ONE OF MY CONTRACT WRITERS STOLE FROM ME.

As one of my side projects before I began my book marketing consulting company, I hired freelance writers to help me put out several online publications. I discovered one day that one of those writers stole money from me by having advertisers pay him directly.

I immediately fired him.

Within weeks he started up a competing publication and purposely poached my readership.

After I heard Zelda's story on RadioLab, this scoundrel came to mind. Even though I had long since shut down that publication, I still had an intense hatred for this guy.

I wrote him a check for $1,000.

I then wrote him an apology note taking full responsibility for everything that had happened—something I steadfastly did not believe and was in fact complete BS.

I put both the check and the letter in an envelope addressed to him and even added the stamp.

Then I gave the envelope to a friend of mine, someone I trusted without reservation, with very specific instructions.

"If I don't send you the finished manuscript of my book by July 30, you put this in the mail."

Not only did I not have a spare thousand dollars to give away, the idea of giving that money and apology to someone I hated still makes my blood boil.

I BRUSHED OFF ALL OF THOSE REASONS, EXCUSES AND ROADBLOCKS THAT RESISTANCE THREW AT ME.

The book flowed easily with my anger driving me.

Not only did I finish the book by July 30, I finished a week early.

My friend tore up the check and, after flailing for half a year, I had a finished first draft of my book after only thirty days of heated work.

While this was obviously a nuclear option to getting a project done, it became a useful way for me to counterpunch Resistance's best blows.

I started looking for ways to set up personal behaviors that I would never want to manifest (rewarding a jerk with my hard-earned money being one of them) in order to drive me to do things that were difficult (finishing a draft of my book).

It's amazing how quickly your mind clears with a doomsday approaching.

LOOKING BACK, THIS WAS A BIG MOMENT FOR ME.

Finishing the first draft manuscript for my first book was a marked point in running down my dream.

Over the years as I built my consultant firm and began writing to get more people to pay attention to my company, this vague dream started coming more into focus.

I realized I wanted to be a success, not just monetarily, but also creatively.

What I really wanted wasn't a bunch of money and a successful business (not that those things aren't important and worth working toward). I wanted to be successful in my creative work too.

My dream had moved from rising up the financial hierarchy—that thing that magazines and newspapers and movies and TV shows are really good at portraying—to another value hierarchy.

This new hierarchy was the realm of real artists—people who value the actual process of taking something inside their heads and bringing it into the world. Those who create art are amazing to me. My dream was really about getting into that "artist" arena and seeing if I could make a name for myself in that tent.

I wanted my writing to start going out in the world and being a part of people's lives. I wanted the perception of me to change.

IF YOU TALK TO LONG DISTANCE RUNNERS, THEY'LL TELL YOU THERE ARE DIFFERENT STAGES TO EVERY RACE.

The mental game has to change as you progress through the stages. Some stages are easy and invigorating. Some stages are devastating and crushing. Some hurt emotionally more than physically. At each step in the process you have to develop a new toolset to overcome them.

This is what I had been doing on this run.

I overcame the early hurdle of not being able to get the business work done. Cutting out all the unessential stuff in my schedule and systematizing things forced me to focus on my work and start getting it done.

However, once I started moving into more creative work like writing, I found that Resistance-generated fear waylaid me. Fear's multiple forms and guises held me back over and over again. I'd find one tool and fix one fear only to have another take its place. My toolset grew as I started to develop an internal structure that would allow me to move forward while being pummeled on all sides by fear. The snow, sleet, and rain kept coming down while I learned how to keep putting one foot in front of the other.

Finishing the first draft of my manuscript beat back fear in a way that nothing else had so far. Of course, like Elizabeth Gilbert promised, fear continues to come on every creative road trip—this book included—but its grip on the steering wheel was forever loosened.

I'VE FOUND MOST SUCCESSFUL ARTISTS WILL BE ABLE TO IDENTIFY THE EPIPHANY MOMENT ALONG THEIR JOURNEY.

They'll be able to point to a particular project where things changed for them. The Resistance fear that constantly kept them flailing and never finishing was vanquished, and it was always different after that.

Once I reached this point, like when I started getting my business work done and when I started publishing articles on my website, I thought it would be smooth sailing.

It was so hard to get past all of these "just getting it done" roadblocks that I thought it would be pretty easy to finish up this book and get it published.

How wrong I was.

I had a whole new stage of the race ahead of me.

One that I didn't even know existed, which is the worst kind of stage.

All of the affirmations couldn't help me overcome this one because this time the negative thoughts were true.

I really wasn't good enough.

"WHAT DO YOU WANT?" CANDACE ASKED ME.

I was standing in my kitchesn, dressed for work, jacket on and computer bag in hand, and I was angry.

A couple of months before this moment, Candace called me at work.

I was in the middle of something, so I let it go to voicemail. But instead of leaving a message, she hung up and immediately called back.

This was our signal to answer the phone.

Candace and I established a deal after I kept screening her. If I was in the middle of something at work, I would let her call go to voicemail and I'd get back to her when I was finished. However, if she hung up and called right back, that meant it was an emergency and I needed to answer.

So when a second call immediately came in, I got worried and answered.

"Hey, hon, what's up?"

"A sheriff just came by the house. He had a subpoena for you."

"What? Why?"

"It's from the IRS. Have you been paying our taxes? Because this says you haven't been paying our taxes and now they're taking us to court."

They were right. I had not been paying our taxes.

Well, I had been paying some of them, but not all of them. Money had been tight for so long and so often that there were months I didn't have enough to make my payments.

To make matters worse, I often ignored the letters the IRS was sending me because I was so scared and ashamed of being so far behind on paying them.

I would just send in a little bit of money in hopes that it would keep them off my back a little while longer.

But that little while longer had finally run out, and it was time for me to actually face this problem I had been letting grow for so long.

After several phone calls and hours on the phone with various representatives of the IRS, I was able to negotiate out of having to go to court, but I needed to pay the $20,000 off that I owed them as quickly as possible.

ALMOST IMMEDIATELY AN AMAZING OPPORTUNITY DROPPED INTO MY LAP.

With this $20,000 debt to the IRS hanging over my head, I needed to figure out a way to dig myself out of this hole.

About a week later one of my clients called me. He was a consultant for financial planning firms across the country. He was working with a new firm that had nine locations around the country, and they all needed new websites.

He wanted to bring my firm in to do all of the work!

He said I would definitely get the contract. All I had to do was fly up to Boston for a day so the owner could get to know me and hear a little about how I worked.

The meeting went great!

They loved me and didn't balk at my price of $30,000. I got a verbal agreement from them and flew home over the moon. I was so excited and so thankful that this had dropped out of the sky and saved me.

A couple of days after I got home, I sent an email following up. I needed to send an invoice for the deposit so we could get started. I didn't hear back, so I followed up a couple of days later. It was a Thursday.

Friday came and went along with the weekend. I was starting to get nervous, so Monday morning I gave them a call. The owner was in a meeting but would call me back later that day.

He never called.

Tuesday morning my client, the one who had brought me in for the project, finally called me. I knew something was wrong as soon as he started talking.

Apparently the owner had a relative who was also a web developer, and when he had heard that they were going to hire someone else, he got his feelings hurt. So the owner decided to give the contract to him instead of me.

I WAS CRUSHED.

And I was angry.

I spent the rest of the day tail spinning into a very dark place. The next morning as I was standing in the kitchen ready to go, and Candace asked me a simple question, I started unloading everything on Candace.

All my fear about the money I owed and anger over this job that would have saved me falling through.

Finally, she stopped and asked that question.

"What do you want?"

This stopped me short.

She was obviously asking a bigger question than just "pay off my taxes" or "make more money." She wanted to know what about this situation was really making me so angry.

I took a deep breath.

"I'm just ready for this to be easy."

At first Candace didn't really get what I was saying.

"You want it to be easy? You mean, so it's not a lot of work?"

"No, no. I don't mind working. I'm sick of struggling. Of churning and pushing and feeling like whatever I am and however hard I work, it's never quite good enough."

THIS WAS IT.

This was the constant feeling I had. I was trying. I had fixed and propped up all of these broken places, and yet it still wasn't good enough.

I didn't mind the work. I actually enjoyed the work. I minded the constant feeling that I wasn't good enough.

It reminded me of a song.

My friend Colleen Wainwright had written a little New Year's song and published a video of her playing it in her robe and shower cap. It was called "The Boulder" and the lyrics were:

Verse:
A New Year is upon us,
　　It's a time of hope and cheer.
A chance to do things differently
　　Than how you did last year.
But change is easy stuff to start,
　　And harder to make stick.
How do you really get things done,
　　Instead of just talking about them like a big fat dick.
The answer isn't resolutions, promises, or hacks.
　　Manilla folders, moleskines neatly piled in stacks.
No, the secret to accomplishment
　　Is using all your will,

To push the cocksucking boulder
    Up the mother fucking hill.

Chorus:
Push the cocksucking boulder
    Up the mother fucking hill,
The cocksucking boulder
    Up the mother fucking hill.
You've always been a loser,
    And you always will until,
You push the cocksucking boulder
    Up the mother fucking hill.

Bridge:
Wishes will not cut it,
    Dreams are pointless too.
If you want to change your life for good,
    There's just one thing to do,
    Thing to do,
    Thing to do.

Chorus:
Push the cocksucking boulder
    Up the mother fucking hill,
The cocksucking boulder
    Up the mother fucking hill.
You've never got it done before,
    And never will until,
You push the cocksucking boulder
    Up the mother fucking hill.

WHY IS IT THAT MY BOULDER WAS
ALWAYS HEAVIER THAN I COULD PUSH?

What was it about me that no matter how many books I read or conferences I went to or new stuff I tried, it always seemed to be just short of good enough?

Of course, my fear was that I would never get there.

Again, I didn't mind the work. I could even handle the struggle and pain if I just knew that it was at some point going to abate. That eventually I would get that cocksucking boulder to the top of the mother fucking hill.

I went to work that day, still angry.

I wasted most of the day not doing much except wallowing in self-pity. The feeling didn't go away. I shoved it down, moved on, and kept working. But that feeling was still there. Resentment…Resistance's diabolical executioner.

This moment in time was the closest I came to abandoning my dream, my all is lost moment…when I hit a very dark pit after reaching a checkpoint (finishing my manuscript) that I thought would solve all of our problems.

It wasn't just the $20,000 I owed the IRS. It was what it represented. When I started this journey I was staring down owing a $576 mortgage payment I couldn't make.

After six years of work, I was now $20,000 in the hole.

I was going in the wrong direction. If I kept up this pace, in another six years I'd be over $690,000 in the hole.

And what was the point of all this? What was I really trying to build? What was I trying to do? Who was I trying to be?

While I had gotten a better handle on what my dream was—I knew I wanted to write and I knew I wanted freedom—I seemed to be no closer to those goals.

I was just sinking more and more into a hole. If I stopped now and got a job, I could start paying back the tax payments and at least know where the money was going to come from.

I CAME ACROSS AN ARTICLE.

TOOL: YOU ARE SUPPOSED TO SUCK

Jason Fried wrote a story for *Inc.* titled "How to Get Good at Making Money". I was a big fan of Jason's. He cofounded a design firm called 37signals in 1999 when he was twenty-five years old. Six years later in 2004 they launched an online project management service called Basecamp. It quickly took off and pretty soon they stopped doing design work and focused all of their time on developing and growing Basecamp. The company has always been profitable and never took outside funding. I respected Jason and how he ran the company for years.

Reading that article changed my life.

In it Jason talked about how he recently began learning how to play the drums.

And, of course, he was really bad at it.

This got him thinking about his journey of learning to make money. For him, it began when he was fourteen years old when he got a job selling tennis and golf equipment. In the article he outlines the ups and downs all the way through launching and growing Basecamp, which was his first real, large success.

It took him seventeen years of practice before he finally learned how to make money.

After reading this article, I sat back in my chair and thought about where I was on my journey.

I had only been at it for six years.

I'm still a beginner, I thought.

Then I thought about the book *Outliers* and Malcolm Gladwell's assertion that it takes ten thousand hours—roughly ten years—of concentrated practice to become a master at something.

"Okay, so maybe I'm intermediate. But I've still got at least four years before I become an expert at this. Before I can really decide that I'm never going to make it."

Then it dawned on me.

"I'M SUPPOSED TO SUCK AT THIS."

If I were learning to play the piano, I wouldn't denigrate myself if I wasn't any good at it when I started. Even after five or six years of practice, I'd be getting better but would be nowhere near as good as someone who had been working at it for more than ten years.

That would be expected.

So why did I quickly shame myself and feel awful because I wasn't already a master at business and writing? These were learned skills too.

This revelation switched my entire attitude toward my work. My job was to stick with it and keep going...to use duct tape and chewing gum if necessary to keep my shoes together...to do whatever was necessary to just keep crawling in the direction I was heading.

Although it was early in the process, I still had a long way to go and a lot to learn, and that wasn't only okay, it's exactly how it's meant to work.

Sure, I still sucked at this and the boulder felt heavier than I could handle, but my job was to simply keep pushing.

"WE'VE GOT HIM IN REHAB DRYING OUT AGAIN."

I paused.

"Okay. Well. Um. Is there anything I can do for you in the meantime?"

"No, I think we're good. I'll have him give you a call once he's out and running again."

I hung up the phone, still a little dumbstruck at the short conversation. I had spent the last couple of weeks trying to get in touch with one of my clients and had finally called one of his employees to track him down. He was a *New York Times* bestselling author and a very popular figure in the online guru space. He was early to the blogging world and had quickly gained a large following around his creativity and unique view on the world.

He was the guy so many of my friends and I wanted to be.

And yet he was in rehab. Again.

After a few minutes, I realized I just needed to add him to my growing list. On the list was another client who was desperately trying to hide his upcoming divorce from his online fans and another *New York Times* bestselling author that was so blocked by the fear of writing her next book that she had missed not one, but two deadlines from her publisher.

I was just surprised.

I knew in an abstract, logical sort of way that all of these eminently more successful people had struggles too, but I still believed at my core that my brokenness was far worse.

I mean, look at what they're accomplishing!

Look at the huge following they've built.

Look at the money they're making.

Look at the books and art and music they're putting out into the world.

I am, meanwhile, sitting in a shithole of IRS debt with the inability to finish any major creative project.

However, the more I worked for these titans of the creative world, the more I came to a world-changing realization.

EVERYONE IS LYING TO ME.

TOOL: EVERYONE IS LYING TO YOU

I didn't get angry about it. I didn't believe it was lying in a malevolent sort of way.

It was just an editing job.

When I read that business book by that successful entrepreneur, besides the opening story about how everything was falling apart, the rest of the book was all of the principles she learned to run, grow, and sell a successful business for a bajillion dollars without any of the hell she went through to learn them.

When I went to the conference and heard the amazing songwriter tell her story, the only real failures she shared were the ones that led directly to the next success not the horrific ones that made her want to pack up and quit the race.

I realized that every successful person has a trail of failures behind them. And not small, "oh that didn't work, but then I found the thing that did!" failures.

No.

They have soul-crushing, years wasted, I-will-never-recover failures.

The business they started grew to a success, and then sank because of their drinking. Oh, and they're still dealing with their drinking. The marriage that unraveled because of their

workaholism, and, while they get invited to speak at conferences all the time, they are really drowning in guilt and would
give back all the success if they could just get her back. Failed
businesses that left the owner in tens of thousands of debt. Re-
lationships that were burned down.

Because here's the true version of everyone's life:

And yet, when they write the book, give the talk or tell
the story, this is the version they tell:

Again, this isn't usually malevolent or just to pump up
their ego. It's because hearing about all of the failures is
pointless. We've all heard the quote from Thomas Edison
about creating the light bulb:

"I have not failed. I've just found the ten thousand ways that don't work."

The truth is, we don't care about the ten thousand failures. We need a light bulb and need the one thing that worked. A book filled with twenty tips that don't work would not sell very well. We want the twenty tips that do work. You can keep the thousand that don't.

Even in this book full of my failures and mistakes, I've had to cut most of them out. Otherwise this book would run well past a hundred thousand words and be a pointless read.

I STARTED TO UNDERSTAND THAT ALL OF THE SUCCESS I SAW AROUND ME WAS THE EDITED VERSION OF WHAT REALLY HAPPENED.

There is no way around failure. We all think we get this, but it wasn't until I hung up the phone after hearing about my client's rehab stint that this sank into my bones.

This running down a dream stuff is really messy. Being compulsive and micro-detail oriented, I thought it through some more.

So if failure is a natural part of the process that is inescapable, how can I do it better?

Who is weathering these failures well instead of sinking into the pit of despair? If I could find those people, maybe I'd get a clue about keeping my head when everything seems to be falling apart.

This is when my mind went to Daniel Pink.

He was one of the first authors I started working with after Ramit Sethi. By this point I had been working with Dan for three years. He already had a couple of *New York Times* bestselling books behind him and I was helping him build up his author platform in preparation of his next book release.

From day one, what amazed me about Dan was his constant assumption that there was probably a better way to do what he was doing. He seemed to step into every situation with a confidence to try something, but also realizing it was probably not the exact right thing.

One time I asked him about this.

"It's all experiments, Tim. It's not about me or my ego or avoiding failure. It's just constantly trying new things to see what works. If I'm wrong, great! I can take that information and jump to the next thing."

This reminded me of one of those things Zig Ziglar said over and over in those recordings I had listened to a few years earlier.

"Failure is an event, not a person."

Dan weathered these failures because he went into everything assuming it would probably fail, but understanding it was just an experiment so he could get to the next thing that had a lesser chance of failing.

WHEN DAN USED THE WORD "EXPERIMENT," MY MIND JUMPED BACK TO MY HIGH SCHOOL CHEMISTRY LAB.

TOOL: EVERYTHING IS AN EXPERIMENT

We had to do all these experiments and then record the results. I wasn't emotionally connected to any of them. That would be pretty weird.

I just dispassionately went through each step of the experimental method.

1. Make observations
2. Form a hypothesis
3. Make a prediction
4. Perform an experiment
5. Analyze the results of the experiment
6. Draw a conclusion
7. Report your results
8. Go back to step 1

What if I started applying this to everything I did?
Literally, everything.
From my parenting and my writing to my hiring and my work with clients?
So I gave it a try.

First, I started actually using this list to make decisions. I found I naturally went through this process anyway, but being very conscious of it allowed me to start seeing things more clearly and start making better decisions about what to do next.

Second, I started constantly reminding myself that what I was working on was an experiment. If it failed, that didn't make me a failure, it made the experiment a failure.

What surprised me the most was how each thing I worked on started having an emotional detachment that I had never experienced before. Instead of my work being this thing inside of me and intertwined with my soul, it allowed me to pull it out and set it on a metaphorical table so I could consider it without tying my self-worth to its success or failure.

This obviously didn't turn me into an emotionless robot that was completely disconnected from the world, but it did allow me to push back from my work in an important way. It allowed me to look at successful people, not with envy, but with an understanding that they were telling me a highly edited version of their story for both of our goods.

It put me in a place where I could learn more easily because my ego wasn't tied up in everything I spent my time doing.

The experimental mindset was a crucial tool I used to move into dealing with that finished first draft of my book.

It had been months since I even looked at it.

SOMEHOW AFTER FINISHING THE FIRST DRAFT, I GOT EVEN MORE SCARED OF THE PROJECT.

I finished the first draft of the manuscript, sent it to my friend so he wouldn't put that $1,000 check in the mail, and then promptly stopped working on the book completely.

It sat on my computer for over a month.

I didn't know what to do next. So I thrashed around thinking about how to deal with failure and Dan Pink's approach to life as a series of experiments. I read Anne Lamott's book *Bird by Bird* and knew that what I had on my hands was a shitty first draft. But I didn't know what level of shittiness it was at or how to identify the shitty parts and make them non-shitty.

I was much too close to the project to make any real decisions.

Plus, being as this was my first book, I was completely inept on what it should be. That is, what category of book it was. Who would care about it. How I should structure it for the people who would care about it. What promise I had to make to get people to pay attention to it. And on and on. These were questions I didn't have answers for. I didn't even know the questions.

I simply didn't know how to start taking this mess of tens of thousands of words and start doing anything meaningful with it.

I NEEDED INPUT ON WHAT TO DO NEXT.

The problem was, I couldn't ask just anyone for input.

First off, most people in my life don't know anything about creative projects. They could read the book, like it or not like it, but not produce any real, concrete feedback that I could use to answer a whole bunch of questions I didn't even know I had to answer. How would they know them either?

Secondly, most people in my life want to make me feel good so they'll default to giving me praise. If I sent the book to my mom, she would just tell me how good it was and how smart I was. Which, admittedly, is nice and empowering, but it's not what I needed in this case. I wasn't making a nice watercolor as a kid and asking my mom to tell me I was a good boy for putting so many interesting colors together.

I needed a handful of people who knew me, knew what I was trying to accomplish, and were willing to tell me the bare, unvarnished truth. I decided early on I'd rather hear how bad my book was from friends, privately, before it was published. That way I could fix it rather than hear from strangers, publicly, after it was published.

Names started popping into my head. Jill. Colleen, from The Boulder song fame. Dan. Gene. Matt.

Five people. That was enough.

I reached out to each of them and made the most irritating and painful ask an amateur creative can ask his friends... will you read the first draft of a book I wrote?

Being good friends, they all agreed to read my shitty first draft and give me advice. I told each of them I needed brutal, unvarnished honesty. I told them each I'd rather hear it from them now rather than publicly later.

A few days went by, and I got the first response. It was a voicemail from Colleen.

"This is so good. It really is great. But you have a lot of work left to do." She then spent several minutes going through her notes. Then she decided it was too much and she would just send them to me.

A few days later I heard from Jill. She also thought I was on the right track, but then let me know that at least a third of the manuscript was useless and needed to be cut. She then went chapter by chapter outlining what was wrong and what needed to be fixed.

I got similar feedback from Gene, Matt, and Dan.

IT WAS DEVASTATING.

I realized that I hadn't really believed I had written a shitty first draft. I thought my draft was probably about ninety percent there and just needed a little cleanup. While I knew I was an amateur creative putting in his ten thousand hours of work to become a craft-wielding pro, my ego thought otherwise. He thought ten thousand hours were for suckers. I'd be able to do that work in half the time…

Now I knew the truth.

I had to cut out at least a third of the book, do an almost complete rewrite of the other two-thirds, and then replace the third I cut with new writing.

I thanked them each for their gracious expenditure of time and their feedback. Then I, once again, stopped working on the book.

This time, it would be five months before I picked it back up again.

IT HAD BEEN SO HARD TO WRITE THE FIRST DRAFT, AND NOW I HAD ALMOST THE SAME AMOUNT OF WORK TO DO JUST TO GET TO A SECOND DRAFT.

TOOL: BUILD A BOARD OF DIRECTORS

It was too much for my psyche to handle.

I didn't say I was too busy. I didn't say I wasn't prioritizing it. I just stopped thinking about it. I acted like the book didn't exist. When people asked me about it, I lied and said I was working on it.

Jill finally nailed me to the ground on it.

She had given me a call and we were chatting about other things. Then she asked me about the book. I tried to obfuscate by saying I was working on it, I thought it was starting to come together, and so on.

But Jill wasn't having it.

"How much more do you have left until a second draft."

"Um, probably about a month?"

"A month? Tim, the book's not that long. What have you been doing the last five months?"

I paused. At this point I was caught in my lie, but I had to figure out if I was going to double down on it or come clean.

I sighed.

"Jill, I haven't touched it in the five months since I got your feedback."

"Why not?"

"It's just so many changes. You made me cut a third of it out. I've got to rewrite the rest plus add a bunch more. I'm worried it's going to take too long."

"Okay, be honest. If you really buckled down and worked on it, how long would it take to get a second draft done?"

I did the rough math in my head and was embarrassed to give the answer.

"A month."

"A month? Really? That's it."

"Yeah. Yeah, I could definitely have it done in a month."

"Then why isn't it done already?"

I paused again, weighing how honest I wanted to be with her, but I figured she'd gone this far with me so I might as well just lay it out.

"What if it still sucks? What if I have to rewrite half of it again? Or, what if I publish it and it's still a disaster?"

"Do you really think I'd let you do that, Tim? You think Colleen would let you get away with that? Or Dan or Gene or Matt?"

"No."

"That's right. You just do the work and trust us. We'll tell you when it's ready."

That was when I realized what these five people represented. They were not just a group of people giving me feedback on my book. They had become my board of directors. I could trust them to tell me the truth, not just about fixing the shitty parts of my book, but also when it was done.

I WASN'T REALLY SCARED OF THE WORK LEFT TO DO ON THE BOOK.

I was scared about churning on it and never knowing when or if it was good enough. I was far too close to the project to make any of the decisions in this area and I knew it.

But Jill helped me realize that figuring out when the book was ready to share wasn't my job.

My job was to do the work and trust the people I had assembled around me to not only keep me on the path, but to let me know when I was finished.

Suddenly, the knot of fear inside of me loosened and I was able to start working again. I woke up the next morning, dug up the notes I had received five months earlier, and started reworking the first draft into the second draft.

Sure enough, I finished it in less than a month and fired it off to my board of directors for feedback.

I WAS BACK ON THE PHONE WITH JILL.

TOOL: FIND AND FOLLOW THE RIGHT MENTOR

It was a few weeks after sending her the second draft. She had gone through the book and made a bunch of notes.

We spent an hour on the phone and only got through about half of the notes. A couple of days later, we got back on the phone. I was expecting to dive right in but Jill stopped.

"I really didn't enjoy our last call," she said.

I was shocked.

"Why? What do you mean?" I asked.

"I've done this for a lot of people and it takes a lot of time, and all you did was argue with me for most of the hour. This whole thing should have taken thirty minutes and we're now going into the second hour. If you trust my advice, then take it. If you don't, find someone you do trust and stop wasting my time."

I glanced down at the notes I had taken and thought back to that first call.

I definitely argued a lot.

She pointed out real problems with my manuscript, and at each point I spent a lot of time arguing with her about why the way I did it was right. The sad thing was, in each instance, I eventually came around to what she was saying.

The truth was, I was so scared my book wasn't good enough that I was fighting any criticism of it.

"Okay," I said. "I'm sorry. I trust you. Let's keep going."

Sure enough, a few minutes later we were done and I had a couple more pages of notes on things I needed to fix in my book. I flipped back through the pages and realized every single piece of feedback was correct.

I thought again about how I had acted on that first call and got a knot in the pit of my stomach. Jill helped many writers with their books. She was a very sharp consultant who had done amazing work over the years. She also used her very valuable time and expertise and was helping me with my book for free.

I had thanked her by arguing and pushing back and, basically, acting like a petulant child when she gave me the criticism I had expressly asked for. Then, as often happens in these moments of realization, I started thinking back to all of the times I had done this before.

Very smart, successful people had tried to help me and I had fought them. Whether it was my own insecurities or ignorance didn't matter. What mattered was I had really smart people trying to help me and I responded like an ass.

Then that self-preservation side of my brain kicked in and I thought of the times over the years I was given some really bad advice. I asked a friend for advice on hiring employees and nothing good happened.

But thinking about it now, I realized my friend had never been in a position to regularly hire new employees.

Then I thought about my super successful client, who was unmarried and had no kids, who gave me some really bad advice on my marriage and parenting.

Then it dawned on me.

MOST PEOPLE ARE AVERAGE OR BELOW AVERAGE AT MOST THINGS, MYSELF INCLUDED.

I'm only really good at a handful of things and have the track record to prove it. However, if you ask my advice on something other than those things I'm expert at, I'll probably still give you advice. People love to give advice, even when they don't know what they are talking about.

As I thought through the bad advice I had received, I realized it was because I had gone to someone who was really good at some things, but not the things I was asking about.

I opened up my laptop and started writing a note to Jill, apologizing for how I had acted and thanking her for putting up with me. I thanked her for taking the time to give me notes on the book. I also promised to never act like that again when I asked for her help.

But I made a much bigger promise to myself in that moment.

The first promise was to only ask advice from experts on things they are experts on. No more trying to find a life coach or a mentor that would help me in all the areas of my life. From now on, when I ran into a problem I needed help on, I would seek out an expert on that subject and only ask them for advice.

Then, once I found that person and they were willing to help me, I made two rules.

First, I'm not allowed to argue or question the advice. The only questions I am allowed to ask are clarifying questions if I don't understand something about the advice they are giving me.

Second, I will do whatever they tell me to do. Unless it is unethical, illegal, or immoral, I will just do it.

Once I started taking this tack with asking for advice, so many good things started happening.

First off, it allowed me to relax and just act. The weight of the decision disappeared. Once the expert told me what to do, all of the stress disappeared. I just did what I was told.

This is what happened with Jill's feedback on the book. Once I started assuming it was right, I didn't have the stress of figuring out what was wrong with my book. I just worked my way through her notes and fixed the things she said to fix.

Second, everything started working better, faster. Even if the advice of the expert was wrong, I stopped getting stuck at the "form a hypothesis" stage of the experiment trying to make the right decision. I just did what I was told and then reported back to get the next thing to try.

I didn't know it at the time, but when I hung up with Jill, I was only a couple of weeks away from having a finished manuscript that was ready for copyediting. By relaxing and trusting the experts, all I had to do was show up and do the work.

All of the decisions about how to make something publishable and worth people's time and money were being made for me.

SOMETHING INSIDE OF ME SHIFTED
WITH THIS REALIZATION.

It wasn't just the decisions to go to the right experts or to take their advice without argument. It was finally letting go of this pressure to have all the answers. I had been holding on to my belief that everything was on me to figure out, know, and get right. I would fight with the people trying to help me because I was scared of being exposed as not knowing what to do.

Of course, this makes no sense.

I asked for help because I couldn't do something in the first place, but then taking their advice without question made me feel like I was stupid and should have already known what they were sharing with me.

But this shift in attitude from Mr. Disagreeable to Mr. Mentee allowed me to start asking for help more and not feeling like I had to get it all right all the time.

I could relax, be the expert on the things I was good at, and let other people be the expert on things they were good at.

Duh.

IN THE MIDST OF THIS NINE-MONTH PROCESS OF IGNORING MY BOOK, I HAD BEEN HAVING ONE OF THE MOST STRESSFUL, YET SUCCESSFUL RUNS IN THE SHORT HISTORY OF MY BUSINESS.

After working with Ramit Sethi, I began working with Daniel Pink, the experimental mindset guy.

He was already a successful author but started working with me to get his online marketing ready for his next book. He knew there was work for him to do there, even though he had already "made it," so he got me involved to help out.

I started working with Dan several months before his bestseller *Drive* came out. And now it had been three years working with him to grow his online platform. We were gearing up for the launch of his next book, *To Sell Is Human*. Six months before, I had nervously taken a train up to see him and his wife Jessica to share my plan for the launch. I'll never forget them approving the plan over a cup of coffee at their kitchen table.

Dan had been paying me for three years, month in and month out, to ensure that he was ready for this moment. I had made big promises on what my ideas and methodology would do for him, and now I desperately needed them to pay off. As Dan's publish date neared, I worked constantly on all the details to prepare for the launch.

I was full bore focused on *To Sell is Human*.

In the midst of this commitment, I got a call from another Dan—Dan Heath.

Dan and his brother Chip had published the wildly successful books *Made to Stick* and *Switch*. They had heard about me and were interested in working with me on the launch of their next book, *Decisive*, which was coming out just three months after Dan Pink's book.

I signed on.

Along with Dan Pink and the Heath brothers, I was helping with the launch of *Salt, Sugar, Fat* by Michael Moss. Michael's book was coming out in between the Pink and Heath launches.

And my client Hugh Howey had sold the print rights for his independently published bestselling novel *Wool* picked up by the publisher Simon and Schuster. They were releasing Hugh's book around the same time as the Heaths.

All four of the major projects were coming together right as Jill was getting on the phone with me and convincing me it was time to finish my book.

Each of the opportunities were too good to pass up, so I agreed to all of it, put my head down, and got to work.

I DON'T REMEMBER A LOT ABOUT THAT STRETCH OF WORK.

A week after publication Dan Pink gave me a call.

To Sell Is Human debuted at #1 on *The New York Times*, *Wall Street Journal*, and *Washington Post* bestseller lists. He was thrilled. He thanked me for all my work, we spoke briefly about next steps, and then we hung up.

I sat in my office and stared at the floor.

I didn't feel any joy after the news.

All I felt was a dark dread creeping up my back.

I thought about the Heath brothers, along with Michael and Hugh. Now they would expect the same thing.

I had to pull this off three more times over the next three months. So, again, I hunkered down and got to work.

My life became a blur of phone calls with publishers and authors, writing marketing copy, building marketing systems, and everything else that went into the day-to-day of my job.

Except now everything was turned up to eleven.

Salt, Sugar, Fat debuted at #1 on *The New York Times* bestseller list. A month later *Decisive* debuted at #2 and *Wool*, a reissue of a book that had previously been published to great success, hit #16 on *The New York Times* bestseller list.

I had a bit of luck that week too.

My client Charles Duhigg, who I had helped launch his book the year before also hit the list for his book *The Power of Habit* and Dan Pink's paperback edition of his previous book *Drive* had just come out and sold enough to also hit *The New York Times* list.

All of this together meant I had five clients on *The New York Times* bestseller list at the same time.

It's hard to express how unlikely it is to have five clients on the most coveted bestseller list simultaneously. For a small-time book-marketing consultant with no experience working at the big publishing corporations and living in rural Virginia, this phenomenon was all but impossible.

Even the big time New York book publicists would be envious of this kind of success.

And yet, I didn't celebrate. I didn't throw a party. I didn't even have a celebratory drink.

DAN HEATH CALLED ME UP.

"We hit #2!" he said.

"Yeah, I saw that…Sorry about that."

"Sorry? Why?"

"Well, we were aiming for #1. That's what *Switch* did."

"We were up against Dr. Phil. What can you expect?"

Dan and I chatted a few more minutes and then hung up. He was thrilled with the results of the launch. So were Michael and Hugh and Dan Pink.

Everybody was happy, except for me.

All I could think about was the fact that we had missed #1 for *Decisive*. Then I thought about my own book that was coming out in two short months and a deeper vein of dark dread crept into my spine.

There was no time to celebrate or even take a deep breath. I had to get back to work.

MY FINAL DRAFT COPY WAS LOCKED.

The copyeditor had it and was working through the first section. I also picked a title for my book. After a lot of back and forth I finally landed on *Your First 1000 Copies*. The cover was being designed. I was getting blurbs.

It was all coming together.

Candace would say later about these last couple of months leading up to the release of my book that I was "insufferable." I think she was being polite. I thought about it constantly. Worried about it constantly.

One day, about six weeks before the book came out, I was walking to lunch with Joseph, one of my employees, and we ran into Matt and Lucas, some friends of ours who worked at a different office in our complex.

I started chatting with Lucas and, of course, telling him about the book.

He asked what the title was. I told him.

Now, Lucas is a thoughtful, soft-spoken fellow. He stood there for a few seconds nodding, and then said, "Well, I hope you sell at least a thousand of them."

Suddenly, my fear and dread spiked even higher than they had already been. He was right!

I knew from working in the industry that the vast majority of books sell only 250 copies in their first year and less than 1,000 copies in the entire life of the book. What if my book didn't even sell a thousand copies? I'd have to retitle the book *Your First 183 Copies*.

Not to mention that I would be the book marketing expert who couldn't market his own book.

So back into the mines I went.

I obsessed over the book and all of the details for the last six weeks leading up to its release. I felt like if I could just get this book launched and doing well, I would be able to take my first deep breath in nine months since I started the sprint of book launches back in the fall.

Finally the day came.

I promoted it to my small audience and sales started coming. It wasn't huge, but they were picking up steam. Every person who emailed me or posted online about the book, I immediately responded to. I obsessively checked my reviews on Amazon.com to see what people thought about the book.

THEN THE SEVENTH REVIEW SHOWED UP ON AMAZON.

It was by an author named Scott Berkun. I didn't know Scott personally, but I did know his work. He was a successful author with several bestsellers and a robust speaking career.

His review of my book read:

"I'm a successful full-time author working on my fifth book. I'm familiar with book marketing experts and methods and sadly promises few authors achieve and are poorly written books of little substance.

"This book is a glorious breath of fresh air. He honestly covers the facts, the methods and the attitudes that have worked for the authors he's worked with. These are not the cheapest or easiest methods to try and he's honest about that. Both he's also clear on the reasons and logic behind why these approaches are worthwhile in the long term.

"It's a short, well-written book—I read it in about an hour. Most of what I feel is regret I couldn't have read this a decade ago when I began writing books."

I couldn't believe it. This wasn't a review from an existing fan of mine. It wasn't a blurb from someone who knew me. It was a real, honest review from a successful author who had no connection to me and no reason to leave a positive review other than truly enjoying the book.

I read the review over and over again.

This was the moment when I decided the book was good. This was the first time I felt like all of that work had paid off, and I could relax and promote the book knowing it would actually help people.

So I kept pushing, and a little over a week into the launch I broke through a thousand copies sold. I was thrilled. I had hit my goal of selling a thousand copies of my book and had received glowing reviews from real writers.

About two weeks after the release of the book, I packed my bags and headed out to Portland, Oregon. I was attending the World Domination Summit, a conference for people seeking to live an unconventional lifestyle. The attendees were people from all over the world trying to start their own businesses, follow their dreams, and spend a weekend connecting with other people like themselves.

A lot of my friends attended the conference every year, and I was looking forward to spending a few days together in one of my favorite cities.

By the end of the weekend, I was wrung out. I had stayed up late every night partying with friends and then was up early for breakfast and coffee with people I needed to spend time with. On the last night of the event, I got invited to a party on the roof of The Nines Hotel in downtown Portland. My friend and client, the bestselling author Pamela Slim, was getting some people together and wanted me there. She was one of the most popular speakers at the World Domination Summit and I was thrilled to be invited.

Once I was there Pam pulled out her copy of my book, threw her arm around me, and posed for a picture.

At the time this picture was taken I had surpassed every goal I had set out in front of me. I had worked with some of the most well-known writers on the planet, helping them with their marketing, and three months before had a run of success that was unheard of in my industry. I had written and successfully launched my own book that was selling well and getting high praise. To top all of that off, I was getting invited to parties thrown by popular, successful people who I had dreamed of being included with.

AND YET, I WAS MISERABLE.

I knew I should be happy. Everything was going my way. I had everything I wanted. In every sense of the phrase, I had been successful in running down my dream.

And look at all I had overcome.

I started out crying on a toilet because I couldn't afford my mortgage, and now I was successful. I had a business turning away clients because we were too busy and I became a real, published writer.

And I still had the check from my mom and dad. I never had to cash it!

So why did I still feel so fucking broken inside?

A new kind of dread settled over me. Not the dread of messing up a book launch for a client or writing a book that failed. This was a deeper, yawning crevasse.

I thought about that movie with Jack Nicholson where he plays an obsessive-compulsive novelist who, through a long series of events, ends up back at his therapist's office. After an unsuccessful interaction on the couch, he walks out into the waiting room, looks around, and then delivers the line that gave the movie its name.

"What if this is as good as it gets?"

I knew there was always more to accomplish. I had more goals in my life. But this dread I was feeling came from the fact that nothing had really changed.

I still felt just as broken as when I started. I was still deeply unhappy.

Shouldn't this stuff be happening on some kind of sliding scale? The more I fixed myself, the happier I should get. The more goals I accomplished, the more whole I would feel. I didn't mind putting in more years and more work, but here I was, sitting on top of the mountain I had fought to climb, and I was the same broken, unhappy person.

Now what was I supposed to do?

BOOK THREE

THE GOLDEN BUDDHA
Finding the Truth

AT THIS POINT I WISH I COULD TELL A STORY ABOUT EMBARKING ON A NEW QUEST TO FIND MYSELF WHERE EVERYTHING STARTED COMING TOGETHER.

The truth is, my life started unraveling at warp speed.

I returned home from the World Domination Summit to my life and work. The life and work I built based on a belief that success in reaching my dream would finally fix this broken thing inside of me.

Now that I realized things were no better off, I started sinking again.

However, this time was different.

I didn't stop working or run out of money. I just started thinking "fuck it" for whatever came along. I had lost the hope that if I could get to this place of success with my ventures I would finally be happy.

I began taking on projects and clients I normally would have passed on. I began working more, working out more, and, generally, trying to pack my time with as many distractions as possible.

What was the point of holding to any standards or structure if it wasn't going to fix me?

AND THEN CANDACE AND I STARTED A
FIGHT THAT WOULD LAST SEVERAL MONTHS.

We weren't constantly at each other's throats, but there was an underlying tension that would regularly boil over into a fight.

This, of course, had been growing long before my trip to Portland. However, after the realization I had there, everything went into overdrive. I had felt broken for so long, but could keep going based on the hope that I would one day be fixed.

That hope had been snuffed out.

I was still a mess even though I had hit the finish line...I ran down my dream and realized that the accomplishment meant little to me.

The summer ended and we rolled into September. I found myself in San Francisco. I had been invited to teach a two-day seminar to a small live audience that would be streamed live to thousands of people all over the world. It was in a studio with three cameras and hosts and a team of a dozen people working only on my seminar.

I was a nervous wreck leading up to it.

I obsessively prepared for my presentation as it approached and drove myself hard leading up to it. I was always nervous before speaking, but this amped it up to a whole new level.

I left for San Francisco, things still tense with Candace, and disappeared into my hole of obsessiveness for the days of the seminar. The seminar went extremely well. The hosts were thrilled with it, the students loved it, but, of course, it only drove me closer to the edge of despair.

The company hosting me threw an after party up on the roof of their building. All I remember is standing on the edge of the roof, beer in hand, staring out over the city and wondering why everyone else seemed to be having such a great time.

The day after the event, I peeled myself out of bed and took a car to the airport. I was flying down to Los Angeles for a couple of days to help a friend of mine with a project he was working on. That evening Candace called me. I stepped out of my friend's apartment to take the call.

To be honest, I don't remember a lot of what Candace said. When I ask her about it, she remembers telling me that she was scared I was heading for a brick wall and desperately wanted me to stop. She felt like I was putting our family in jeopardy, and she couldn't stand around and allow that to happen to us or our children.

ALL I REMEMBER IS THE FEELING THAT I WAS STEPPING OUTSIDE OF MY BODY AND LOOKING AT MYSELF FOR THE FIRST TIME.

I finally saw that this despair I was slipping into was sending me down a path that was going to leave me not just broken but alone.

I began blubbering my sorries to Candace and told her I didn't know what to do, but for her to think about what she wanted from me and I would do whatever she said. I was far too lost to make any decisions about what to do next, so all I could do was rely on her to point me in the right direction.

Two days later I flew home, we sat down at the kitchen table, and she pulled out the list she had made. There were several small things on the list that were easy to agree to, but the big one was to start seeing a therapist.

Candace had started seeing a therapist soon after our second son Maxwell was born, so this was not a big deal for her.

For me, I was accustomed to her being the one needing therapy and assuming I was fine.

That was now turned upside down.

I got a referral from her therapist and sat down with him for our first meeting. He asked me a lot of questions, pushed me on some things, and then, at the end of the session, turned to his desk and started making notes.

"So you want to come in next week again and we can get to work?"

"Um, sure. But what do you think? Do you think I need this?"

He spun his chair back to me and cocked his head to the side.

"Oh yeah, you got problems."

I learned right then and there that this therapist was known for his bluntness.

"But that's okay," he continued. "That's why you'll come back next week."

He handed me a stack of papers to work through as my homework and sent me home. I did the homework and turned them in the following week during our session.

BY THE THIRD SESSION, HE HAD
ASSESSED THE INITIAL HOMEWORK.

TOOL: GET A THERAPIST

Every therapist has their own kind of methodology for assessing and working with patients. For this guy, he broke everything into five categories.

"How'd I do?" I asked, nervously trying to joke around before I heard the verdict.

He held up a piece of paper with the five categories.

"In these four," he said, "you're doing okay. But in this one," he pointed to the one in the middle, "you're clinical."

"Clinical? What does that mean?" I asked.

"People locked up in mental clinics—you're like them. The only reason you're not locked up is because you've figured out how to use these other four areas to compensate."

"Oh," I said. I paused for a bit. "So what now?"

"Now, we get to work."

MY LIFE BECAME FITS AND STARTS AND STOPS OF PROGRESS, REGRESSION, THEN SOME MORE PROGRESS.

It was just like a big nasty project...only the project this time was sorting myself out.

Most of my time was spent with the feeling that I was sitting in a dark cave with no source of light. I had the distinct feeling that something awful was going to find me and devour me. Unfortunately, there wasn't much to do because if I got up and started trying to walk through the cave, I was sure to get hurt in the complete darkness.

The only thing I could do was wait for the light to come as I heard the monsters prowling around me in the dark.

After a decade of constantly working and working and pushing and pushing, I finally decided it was time to stop cranking on external goals. If I kept running when I couldn't see anything, I was only going to keep hurting those closest to me and myself.

I had fixed so many things in my behavior. I was working steadily and getting things done. My business was growing and doing well. My writing was coming along and I was even working on my next book.

All of these external things had been fixed, but I realized the inside of me was still a broken mess. Anytime I looked in there, it was only darkness.

And so I waited.

I kept working. I kept seeing my therapist. I decided that my path had only led me toward a despair that was going to eat me alive, so my job was to stop, put myself in the hands of people I trust, and wait for the answer to come.

It was slow. It was hard. It was scary.

But the answers began to come.

THERE ARE ALWAYS HEALTHY AND UNHEALTHY SIDES TO EVERYTHING.

When my therapist diagnosed me with obsessive compulsive personality disorder, I got freaked out. I didn't know what it meant, but it didn't sound good.

It's like when your doctor gives you the fancy medical name for what he's found and you assume that any word with that many consonants must mean cancer.

When I expressed this fear, he said, "Hey, it's not always bad. It means you'll actually do whatever I tell you to do. Some of my other patients could use a bit of obsessiveness. It could help them make some progress."

ONE OF THE WAYS I OBSESS OVER SOMETHING IS WHEN I FIND A NEW BOOK I LOVE OR HEAR AN INTERVIEW THAT RESONATES WITH ME, I'LL SPEND THE NEXT MONTH CONSUMING EVERYTHING THE AUTHOR HAS EVER CREATED.

TOOL: CONSUME EVERYTHING

I'll listen to every interview they've done, read all their books and articles, and watch every video.

A few years before I made it to the couch, I obsessed over Dallas Willard's work. He was an American philosopher who spent most of his career teaching at The University of Southern California. He translated many of the German philosopher Edmund Husserl's works (the founder of phenomenology) into English and wrote extensively in the Christian tradition.

In one of Willard's pieces, he talked about the importance of separating effort from earning. He said our job was to work as hard as we could and then "leave the result up to God."

As with most things, this didn't sink in the first or third time I heard it. This idea seemed so foreign to me.

What was the point of putting in any effort if it wasn't to earn something? I worked to make money to pay for things. I wrote books to grow my fame so I could get more clients and sell more books.

It wasn't until I read another of Steven Pressfield's books that it began to make sense.

IN *THE AUTHENTIC SWING* PRESSFIELD DESCRIBES THE WAY HE RIFFED ON THE ANCIENT HINDU SCRIPTURE, *BHAGAVAD GITA*, AS THE BASIS FOR HIS BOOK *THE LEGEND OF BAGGER VANCE*.

Being the obsessive compulsive that I am, this prompted me to take a look at this Hindu scripture Pressfield was so enamored with. I found this line:

"You have a right to perform your prescribed duties, but you are not entitled to the fruits of your actions."

Reading this line helped me recall Willard's teaching on separating my effort from my earning.

What are the chances that three very different philosophical approaches for dealing with how to behave in this very complex world—one thousands of years old, one from the early twentieth century and one from a contemporary Christian philosopher—relied upon similar fundamental approaches to work without there being something to it?

Pretty slim, I suspect.

So what if I started doing the work for the work's sake instead of doing the work to get something?

What if my job wasn't to toil for reward but to toil for the love of the toiling?

This forced me to start reconsidering what my work was.

THE FIRST THING I DID WAS TO START SEPARATING WORK I DID FOR MONEY AND WORK I DID FOR WORK.

Even though I ran my own company, I started a new way at looking at things.

I started cheating on my day job.

Instead of bending everything toward my company and clients and making money, I started doing side projects for fun.

I had a few rules for them though.

First, I had to consider them more than hobbies.

This wasn't just something cool I wanted to learn how to do. I had those too, but this was something I felt ran deeper for me. It had to come from that place inside of me that was still dreaming. The thing that pressed me to keep crawling forward.

Second, I wasn't allowed to put any external pressure on myself about "results." I only worked on these projects as much as I felt like and I had no goals around them.

I wasn't trying to accomplish anything per se. I just created space for these things in my life to see what would grow out of them. Or what wouldn't grow. No matter.

The first amazing thing that came out of this was, to my surprise, I actually started working on some things that I'd always put off as "someday I'll do that thing" kind of dreaming.

I began writing fiction for the first time. I wrote things that I just wanted to get down on paper with no plan to ever publish them.

AT THE NEXT WORLD DOMINATION SUMMIT, I MET MY OLD BUSINESS COACH JOSH KAUFMAN FOR A DRINK.

He had stopped being a business coach for a while now, but we had remained friends and always grabbed any opportunity to see each other.

In that meeting I told him what my strategy was anytime I started to reach a goal in my life. I would just push the goal further back. I felt like the only way I could motivate myself was to constantly keep the goal out of reach. Then I would guilt myself into continuing to work toward the new goal.

This often looked like finding someone else who was more accomplished than me and shaming myself for not being as good as them yet.

Whether it was in business, acquiring "freedom," or my personal life, anytime I found myself reaching a new goal I had set in my life, my mind would immediately find someone else who was more accomplished than me and set the new goal there. My business was okay, but not as good as my buddy Mike's. My freedom was solid but nowhere near as free as as that famous blogger's. My family stuff was stabilizing but it was in no way as fulfilling as that guy in my men's group.

In that conversation Josh asked me, "What if you stopped now and never accomplished anything else? Would that be okay? Could you be happy with that?"

I'm not sure how I responded, but I remember being extremely confused.

Of course I couldn't be happy with what I had accomplished.

I had way too much to do!

And how would I ever motivate myself to get anything done if I actually thought what I had accomplished was enough? I would slip right back into that lazy loser from seven years ago who never got anything done.

Josh's words didn't make any sense to me then. But they started to after I'd opened up this tiny pocket in my life where I gave myself permission to accomplish nothing with it.

It was only there for me to run down dreams that had no finish lines or external expectations of satisfaction. And yet, I worked on these tangential projects with vigor. I stopped worrying about when or if spoils would follow.

I merely worked for the sake of working, and it was wonderful.

THIS SMALL CHANGE BEGAN SHIFTING MY MOOD TOWARD ALL MY WORK.

I started trying to think of all the work that included running errands, buying groceries, and making money as external work—work that we did only for the spoils.

Then I viewed all the work that was my art and creativity as my internal work—work that I didn't have the right to the spoils.

But what about everyone else's spoils?

They looked so good!

It often made me question if my external work was the right work.

There's a curse in today's world of endless opportunities. No matter what I pick, it's too easy to find examples of why I may be picking the wrong thing.

I saw other people in my space launching book after book to the bestseller lists, putting on successful events, and traveling the world getting paid to speak. I was scratching out a living as a book marketing consultant in Middle-of-Nowhere, Virginia.

I knew there was always a backstory and everyone had their demons, blah blah blah, but I kept believing that if I could just be more like these people, I would be more successful.

I would hear an interview with some famous online guru and try to mimic their morning routine. Or I'd read a well-researched, highly footnoted book and denigrate my own books that were merely based on my experience. Or I'd read about a family that sold everything and bought an RV to travel the world, and feel lame because the longest trip we'd ever taken was a week.

Soon after publishing my book, I was at a conference and met Scott James. He had been reading my writing for a while and we had traded some emails, so it was fun to meet face to face.

I often felt inadequate when I corresponded with Scott because he wrote poetry, and I never quite knew what to tell him when it came to marketing advice. No matter how you sliced it, poetry just wasn't in high demand in our current culture.

We stood there chatting for a few minutes and then he invited me to a party. He told me he'd have his typewriter set up and would be writing poetry on the spot for people. When I showed up, I noticed a line at a table in the back. When I got over to take a look, I saw Scott sitting at a table with an old, mechanical typewriter, banging out poetry. He would ask the person in front of him a few questions and then type up a small verse for them on the spot.

It was amazing to watch.

Later on we were chatting again, and I asked him if he ever wrote anything else.

"What do you mean?"

"Well, poetry is hard to sell. Have you thought about writing anything else?"

Scott looked a bit confused at first, and then he shrugged.

"I'm a poet."

I didn't know how to respond.

I SPENT MOST OF MY TIME TRYING TO FIGURE OUT WHAT OTHER PEOPLE WANTED (THE MARKET) SO I COULD FIX SOMETHING INSIDE OF ME IN ORDER TO GIVE IT TO THEM.

It never occurred to me that, like it or not, I was already something.

I realized in that moment with Scott that I spent most of my time being envious of other people's callings. I kept thinking if I could just mimic what other successful people were doing, I could also mimic their success.

I never thought about the possibility that their success was rooted in merely expressing what was inside of themselves all along.

I believed what was inside of me was broken and untrustworthy. They didn't. Pretty interesting.

I thought I was broken because of all the horrible and damaging mistakes I had made along the way. Obviously I had a screw loose inside of myself that caused me to botch everything I touched. It seemed like anytime I wasn't white knuckling my life, it would immediately start falling apart.

Yet, the more people I met who were truly happy in their work, the more I saw the pattern that they simply seemed to rest and wait for what was inside of them to come out.

If this is true, what did that say about me?

I had to decide if I believed I was the one truly broken person on the planet, or maybe this idea that I was inherently broken was holding me back.

IN 1767 THE BURMESE ARMY INVADED THE CAPITAL OF THE SIAMESE KINGDOM.

The city of Ayutthaya was located in modern day Thailand. Soon after the assault, the Siamese Kingdom fell, and the people abandoned the decimated city and ventured into parts unknown to rebuild their civilization

Over the ensuing fifteen years, the Siamese people recovered from the war and reformed a central government. In 1782, Phra Phutthayotfa Chulalok, also known as Rama I, put down the final oppositional conflict and established the new Rattanakosin Kingdom. He became its first king and established the capital city Rattanakosin, or what we now know as Bangkok.

A few years later, as part of the reconstruction process, Rama I began building lots of temples in his new capital city. He dispatched emissaries out to the cities that had been ruined in the war to bring back any statues of Buddha that they could find to be housed in his new temples.

One of these Buddha statues was recovered from the ruined city of Ayutthaya.

While this Buddha was impressive in size, standing over ten feet tall, it was a mess.

It was worn down by the years of neglect and made of a primitive stucco substance, a primordial kind of plaster, and covered in layer upon layer of guano. When it first arrived in Bangkok, it was dumped at the Wat Chotanaram temple and soon forgotten.

The Wat Chotanaram eventually fell into disrepair too, so in 1935 the massive glob of goo was moved to the Wat Traimit temple. The problem was that the Wat Traimit temple didn't have room for such a large, unkempt statue, so the brothers just stuck it outside under a tin roof.

Twenty years later, in 1955, they built a new monastery on the temple grounds large enough to hold this all but forgotten Buddha. They hooked up ropes and pulleys and started the delicate process of moving this five-ton behemoth across the temple grounds and into the new building.

At the end of the process just as they were about to get the monster Buddha into the building, the ropes snapped and the statue landed with a loud crack.

Since it was late and these poor monks had been working all day to move this ugly statue, they decided to quit and deal with the mess the next morning.

That night, one of the monks came out with a flashlight to check on the statue. When his light flashed across the Buddha, he noticed a yellow glint come from deep in one of the cracks.

He chipped away part of the plaster and found gold underneath.

All the next day the monks chipped away at the crust.

What they found underneath was the most beautiful, ornate, and valuable Buddha statue that had ever existed.

This solid gold Buddha statue, worth over $250 million dollars, now sits in an extension of the Wat Traimit temple that was built specifically to house and display this impossibly beautiful and ornate artifact. It has become the most beloved and visited statue in the world.

Way back in the 1700s, due to outside threats, monks covered the Buddha. Not to hide the beauty, but to protect it from danger. And then everyone forgot there was something remarkably valuable underneath the grungy facade.

SOMEWHERE, EARLY ON, I PICKED UP THE BELIEF THAT I WAS BROKEN.

I often thought of myself like one of those old broken statues you see with the scaffolding built around them in order to keep them standing. I dedicated years of my life, considered it my job in life even, to build a scaffolding around myself in order to keep me from falling apart.

Obviously, if I was broken, I couldn't trust anything that came from inside of me. Emotions, thoughts, and desires were all to be mistrusted. If the source is tainted, you can't trust anything that comes from it, right? Garbage in, garbage out.

I searched for new and better ways to build a stronger, more secure scaffolding around myself to hold me together. I built new rules and systems. I consistently shamed myself and pushed myself to be better. This was all driven out of a fear that if I let go or relaxed, everything would unravel quickly.

After all, I'd proven what a mess I was, hadn't I?

Look at what I did when I quit my job to work for myself. I was lazy and procrastinated and ended up running out of money and putting my family at risk. And look at how I avoided my taxes, which brought a sheriff to our front door, and look at how I almost destroyed my marriage.

At each step in the process, my assumption was that I hadn't built a strong enough structure around my brokenness and it was starting to leak out. So I drove myself harder, obsessed about it more, and gripped tighter onto control.

However, evidence was starting to mount that I might be wrong. I kept running into people like Scott who projected a fundamental ease about himself that I didn't possess. Of course, I had always had these people in my life, but as I became more exhausted, I started noticing them more.

And then I attended a conference where the speaker shared the story of the golden Buddha, and it all clicked for me—the paradox that I needed to build the scaffolding not to keep me standing, but to chip away all of the plaster that was covering me.

My scaffolding, my tools, weren't holding up my ridiculous broken-down wreck of a self. They were the chisels and hammers cracking the plaster on top of the self I needed to put forth into the world.

SO WHAT IF I CHANGED MY FUNDAMENTAL ASSUMPTION ABOUT MYSELF?

Instead of "I am broken and in need of fixing," I could start believing "I have a valuable, powerful, perfect force within, and I have everything I need to release it. There are just some layers on top of the gold that I need to scrape away."

What if I started letting go a little bit and trusting what was inside of me without expecting a slap on the back or a check?

The truth is, I always felt like I was hanging on by my fingernails anyway.

What's the worst that could happen? I had shown that all of the white knuckling didn't change anything long term. I kept running into more and more problems. And even when I did reach success, I felt just as broken.

So taking the experimental mindset, I decided to test out a new theory.

First, I would start assuming I was good and had my heart in the right place, instead of a rickety monster that had to be held in check and put on a tight leash.

Second, anything I did that was bad or wrong or unhealthy, I would just tell myself it was a layer of plaster on top.

That wasn't really me. Therefore, changing the behavior wasn't so threatening.

Third, I would only worry about scraping away layers. I was done trying to be a good father, writer, husband, friend, or businessman all at the same time.

If I stuck to my single-minded pursuit, all of that stuff would take care of itself. I never felt good enough anyway even when I thought I was under control.

Instead I would just worry about this one thing... scraping away the plaster.

ONCE I STARTED DOWN THIS PATH, I REALIZED HOW DEEPLY INGRAINED MY "BROKEN MESS" WAY OF THINKING WAS.

Anytime I did anything bad, wrong or unhealthy, I felt like it fit. Because I was broken. Except now, when I caught myself thinking that way, I would stop and think, "No, I'm not broken. That's just a layer on top. I'm valuable and powerful and perfect and have everything I need inside of me."

Of course, nothing changed immediately.

I first had to go through the agonizing period of realizing just how often I thought about myself as broken and how it drove so much of my life.

The way I approached everything had to start changing. If I overslept instead of getting up to write, I assumed it was because I needed some extra sleep, not because I was a loser who couldn't ever consistently get out of bed. If I got stressed about leaving the house late in the morning and yelled at Conner and Maxwell, I would just apologize to them and tell myself that I really wasn't the type of person to yell at my kids. That was just a layer on top.

Everything in me fought this. I felt lazy again. I felt selfish for only thinking of how things affected me.

Resistance to change is as powerful as Resistance to creative effort. In fact, change is creative effort. It's pulling an idea out of our heads and then actively behaving according to that idea.

There were so many times I wanted to revert back to the old way of thinking. Sure, I hated myself. But the old way felt safe. But I had committed to the experiment, so I decided to stick it out until something bad really happened. If I wanted to work on something, I'd work on it. If I didn't want to, I wouldn't. I just kept assuming whatever was coming from inside of me was good.

Sure, I'd hit the snooze for a couple of mornings, but then I would get up and get some writing done. Or I'd just find time later in the day to write. When we were running late, I started assuming I would be fine instead of stressing out. I started working on the things I wanted to work on instead of worrying that I wasn't doing the right things at the right time.

I STUCK WITH IT FOR MONTHS, CONTINUALLY WAITING FOR THE BOTTOM TO FALL OUT AND MY EXPERIMENT TO FAIL, AND YET, IT DIDN'T.

Then I started noticing some weird things.

My work was still getting done. Not only that, it was some of the best work I'd ever produced.

I was even doing the really shitty work like taxes and making phone calls without so much internal drama. It started being weeks and then months without me yelling at the kids or picking a fight with Candace.

The crazy thing was I wasn't trying consciously not to pick fights or yell or any of those things. I just wasn't really doing them anymore.

And then one day I realized I wasn't even trying to think of myself as good anymore. I just believed it.

Of course I flew off the handle a couple of times, but nothing crazily disagreeable like I'd done before when I had that nasty broken guy inside me chained to a radiator.

But when I did lose my cool now, I would just notice it, think some about where that layer of plaster might have come from, and then metaphorically chip it away a little in my head and move on.

IT WAS A THURSDAY MORNING AND I WAS GOING THROUGH MY USUAL ROUTINE.

I pulled into the parking garage next to my gym at 10:45 a.m., but instead of getting out of the car, I sat still for a few moments. Then I started sobbing.

I couldn't help it.

It just came welling out of me out of nowhere. This definitely wasn't the first time I found myself crying alone in the car, but something was different about this.

All I felt was gratitude.

And fulfillment.

And that what I was doing meant something.

It felt like it was overflowing from my chest and I couldn't hold it back.

I sat there crying and thinking.

Thinking about the shame of asking my parents for money. Of the embarrassment of having a sheriff show up at my house. The constant stress of not making payroll. The fear of not creating anything meaningful. And of course, that moment at the rooftop bar in Portland when I had everything I wanted and was miserable.

But all of those moments had lost their power over me.

I realized, in that moment, I'd given Resistance a hell of a fight so far. While he was in no way down for the count, he was hurting and covering up.

The strangest thing was that if you followed me around and watched my life, nothing was all that different. I still had all the same responsibilities. I still struggled to get my work done. I still had to rely on systems to accomplish things. I still had to wrestle to keep fear's hands off the wheel. I still struggled to finish my writing projects. I still relied on mentors and my board of directors. I still have to make worry lists when I get overwhelmed.

But I no longer had that wild-eyed desperation of the last guy stumbling through a marathon hoping that I would eventually cross a finish line that would make me whole. I started with the assumption that at the end of running down my dream I would find the prize. I would find success. I would be fixed. I would be happy.

What I realize now was when I first laced up my shoes, I already had all of those things. The running wasn't about the race or the finish line. It was about the joy of the gift of having something to run after.

I realized the Truth.

There is no finish line. There is no success or failure. There is nothing to fix. There is only the perfect me, my dream, and the joy of running it down.

APPENDIX

Here is a list of the bootstrapping tools I discovered and learned from extremely helpful mentors throughout my transition from video game playing slacker to relatively stable responsible creator.

I've also added some of the books that have inspired my way of thinking along the way.

TOOL NUMBER 1
FIND THE SHORTEST PATH

My favorite scene in the movie *Fight Club* is when Brad Pitt's character, Tyler Durden, drags the convenience store clerk out of the back of the building in the middle of the night and puts a gun to his head.

After some back and forth, Tyler smacks him on the head with the gun and yells, "What did you want to be, Raymond K. Hessel?"

Raymond eventually stammers out, "Veterinarian! Veterinarian!"

Then Tyler says he's going to check up on him.

"If you're not on your way to being a veterinarian in six weeks, you will be dead."

How clear do you think Raymond K. Hessel's focus became? Do you think silly things like time and money got in the way?

Resistance loves to find new and novel ways to distract us from what we need to do. Oftentimes these things feel like work. They feel important.

In my story, I needed more clients. I started thinking about buying advertising and writing guest articles. The former involved spending money I didn't have and the latter involved a long lead time when I had nine days of runway.

Matt helped me see the most direct path to my goal.

What is the most direct path to your goal? What is the shortest path between A—where you are—and B—where you want to be?

Play around with scenarios like mine. If you were out of money and had a week to do something, what would you do? Or if Brad Pitt showed up and put a gun to your head, and you had to make progress, what would you do?

TOOL NUMBER 2

STOP DOING EVERYTHING

When you stop doing the nonessential stuff, you realize that you've got a world of time on your hands. That time is yours to reconfigure to move you forward toward your aspiration. You will never truly understand how much time is yours until you strip away the nonessential.

TOOL NUMBER 3

HOW TO STOP DOING EVERYTHING…LITERALLY

We can all nod our heads when we read tool number two and "get it." But we have to go even further than that to really "get it" at a molecular level.

This exercise is meant to shock us out of the status quo. It's a way to force us to tell ourselves the truth. If you want to find every single way you are wasting time in your life, spend a week cutting out the unessential.

Here's the exercise:

1. List out everything that you do in a day. All of it. Get as granular as you can.

2. Circle everything that is essential. Here are my criteria for what is essential. First, you would die or get extremely sick if you didn't do it—i.e., going to the restroom, taking your medication. Second, it is an extremely important obligation—i.e., going to work or taking my kids to school. Watching TV is not essential. Reading the news is not essential. Having coffee with my friends is not essential.

3. Cross out everything else left on the list.

4. For five days, Monday through Friday, only do the circled items.

5. Each day of the exercise, write in a notebook that only you have access to what it feels like to live like this.

6. After five days, evaluate. Decide what crossed out things you should add back in, and what stay out permanently. Some of the things you lived without for five days you'll want to keep out permanently. Did you enjoy not being on social media or reading the news? Other crossed out things you will add back in, but you will do it decisively. You will decide you want to do these things instead of passively let them creep back in.

7. Do this exercise once a year. Resistance is insidious. It is slow but deliberate. Like the ivy that is beautifully and slowly growing around a tree and choking the life out of it. You must regularly reevaluate what you are spending your time on and where it is going.

CREATE SYSTEMS FOR THE ESSENTIAL

Our life isn't just crowded with unessential stuff. It's also crowded with the essential stuff of life. Paying bills, day job, getting gas in the car, packing lunches, etc. It too quickly crowds our life and chokes out our creative drive.

By creating systems for these essential elements of life, you can spend less mental energy on them and even pass them off to other people to do.

You create systems so things happen automatically. There's a few reasons this is an important step to start taking.

First, and foremost, systems save time. By putting your keys in the same place every day or cooking the same thing for breakfast every morning, you save time in planning, preparation, and doing. You never lose your keys. You always know what you need at the grocery store, etc.

Second, systems save mental energy. You no longer have to decide what to do. Your system takes care of it for you. Also, you stop forgetting to do things because your system always tells you what to do next.

Third, systems set you up for future success. Once you find a good way to do something, you keep doing it that way over and over so you know it will work.

Here's the trigger: Anytime you find yourself doing the same thing over and over, you should turn it into a system.

There are three types of systems you can create.

First, if it's very simple (a handful of steps, like your car keys), merely make a decision on what you are going to do and start doing it that way every time.

Second, for more complex tasks, create a detailed step-by-step checklist.

Every week, after recording the audio for my online radio show, I have twenty-six different things to do to get it ready to send to the editor. They're all simple. Most of them only take a few seconds. However, it was causing me a lot of trouble because I kept forgetting to do different parts of the process.

This would waste my time, cause me to do redo work, and, overall, added stress to what should be a very simple process.

So I created a checklist. It has every single step of the process from the time I start until the time I email the editor with the files. Having the checklist ensures I don't forget an important step. It reduces my average time to completion from thirty minutes to just over ten minutes, and, if I ever hire an assistant to help me, I have the entire process mapped out for them.

Whenever you have a task that you must do repeatedly, and it has more than a handful of steps, you should create a step-by-step checklist that you can follow.

Third, outsource to a computer, service, or person.

I really wanted to start eating a healthier lunch. I had tried taking my lunch to work, but I kept forgetting to bring it with me or didn't plan ahead, so I would end up either going hungry or picking up fast food.

So I outsourced it. I found a service that prepares healthy meals, and they drop them off every Monday morning at my gym. After I work out on Mondays, I grab my meals, put them in the fridge at my office, and my lunches are done for the week.

I've created a system that allows me to completely stop thinking about what I'm going to eat for lunch.

Another way to approach this is to get computers to do things for you.

The thing I hate the most about running my business is all of the payroll and tax preparation. I don't mind paying the taxes so much as filling out the paperwork, sending in payments, and keeping track of all of it. Up until recently, I was doing it mostly by hand. Every two weeks I would write the check for payroll. I'd then go to the state and federal websites to pay my taxes. And then I would fill out the paperwork by hand and send it in.

I had a checklist to make sure I got it all done and turned in the right way, but it was still an annoying and time-consuming process.

Then I found the ultimate online service. They do it all for me. Every two weeks they automatically grab the money out of my business account, direct deposit my check into my personal account, pay all the tax payments, and file all the paperwork. I've found an online service that completely takes care of my checklist for me.

I work out on the same days, at the same times every week. I have a checklist to make sure I pack my workout bag with everything I need in the morning.

I have essential items like toilet paper and deodorant automatically delivered every month to my house.

I leave the house and come home at the same time every work day.

By creating systems, you reduce the time and mental overhead on the essential things you must do, but are not your creative work. You will reduce the amount of time it takes to do these essential tasks while freeing up your mind to focus on your creative work.

TOOL NUMBER 5
DECIDE ON YOUR GOAL–THE 3 F'S

What is driving your work?

Fortune? You don't care about being in the spotlight. You are just focused on building something that brings in money.

Fame? Is it more about becoming known and seen for your work?

Freedom? You want less responsibility more than you want money and fame?

You can get more than one, but only one will drive you. When push comes to shove and you have to choose one over the other, which would you pick?

This isn't a good/bad decision. One isn't better than the other. But knowing what drives you will help you make your decisions easier and quicker in the future.

TOOL NUMBER 6
SCHEDULE CREATIVE TIME

Put your creative time in your calendar and treat it as one of the most important things you do with your time. I used to tell Candace, "Unless someone is bleeding or dying, I won't be answering the phone."

You don't have to tell people it's your creative time. If a client or boss or friend asks for that time, just tell them you have something else scheduled then and offer a different time.

The space for creativity doesn't just happen. You have to plan for it.

TOOL NUMBER 7
CREATE FOR ONE

If you try to create something that everyone will love, you will either create something bland and boring, or, like me, you will be hopelessly blocked.

Focus on a single person you are trying to wow or help, and create something they will love. If one person loves it, plenty of others will too.

TOOL NUMBER 8
SEEK OUT REJECTION

Play the Rejection Therapy Game for thirty days. The only rule is "You must be rejected by another person at least once, every single day."

TOOL NUMBER 9
FIND THE RIGHT KIND OF CRITICISM

Ignore 99.9% of criticism that comes your way. My rule: I only accept criticism from people I know care about me.

Ignore online criticism. Ignore anonymous criticism. Ignore emails that random people send you. Ignore book reviews.

Instead, focus on the handful of people who love you and are willing to tell you the truth. Seek out criticism from them and trust them implicitly.

TOOL NUMBER 10
CREATE A WORRY LIST

If every time you sit down to create, your mind crowds in with all of the worries in your life, it's time to make a worry list.

First, write down every concern, worry, and fear that is on your mind. All of it. Whether it's needing to pay your taxes, washing the dishes, or a marriage that is on the rocks. List it all out.

The list must be exhaustive. If something pops in your head, put it down. There is no filter here.

Second, write at the bottom of the sheet of paper, "All of these things are important and I promise to concern, worry, and fear over them as soon as I'm done with my work." Then set the paper aside, but in easy reach.

Now, get to work.

While you are working, two things are going to happen.

First, the things you have written down will pop into your head to distract you. Simply look at it in your mind and say "I've got you written down. I'll worry about you as soon as I'm done working."

Second, things you forgot to write down will pop into your head. When they do, pick your writing utensil back up, add it to the bottom of the list, read the note you wrote yourself at the bottom of the page, and get back to work.

Once you are done working, read over the list, and then throw it away.

TOOL NUMBER 11
THE MAGIC WAND

If you're a pessimist like me, it's often hard to dream big. There are some up sides to this, but often it keeps us from reaching the things we really want.

So before you start a new project or if you're really stuck in the weeds on a current one, pull out your magic wand and wave it around a little bit.

Sit down with a pen and paper and start dreaming. If you could wave a magic wand to make everything go perfectly and get everything you want in the next five years, what would that look like? What would you have accomplished? Who would you be? What would it feel like? Put it all down. Even the silly stuff and the stuff you just know will never happen.

TOOL NUMBER 12
MAKE FAILURE EXTREMELY PAINFUL

This is the nuclear option. Only use it occasionally for big projects. Otherwise you will drive yourself crazy and potentially fund some very bad people.

That said...the first thing you must do is come up with a clear, concrete version of "done."

Is it when you've sent your manuscript to the publisher? Is it when you've played your three new songs in front of a crowd of at least a dozen strangers? Is it when you've finally released that photography project on your website?

Whatever it is, you must make it so it's clear when you have accomplished it.

Second, pick a date.

The trick here is to pick a timeframe that you can definitely get it done in, but adds a bit of stress. No wishful thinking here. Take a hard look at your schedule, your life, and your project, and decide how long it will take you to finish. Then pick a date on the calendar.

Third, pick an extremely painful consequence.

This has to be something that will really hurt if it happens. Will you send $1,000 to the political party you despise? Will you lose access to your car for a month? Will that picture of you in your underwear get posted online?

It has to be something that mortifies you at the thought of it happening. It has to be big.

Fourth, give away control of the consequence. Pick a friend who is ruthless enough to follow through, and give them control of the consequence with their sworn oath that they will follow through if you don't hit your deadline.

Fifth, get to work.

TOOL NUMBER 13
REALIZE YOU ARE SUPPOSED TO SUCK

This is a mantra to remember.

"I'm supposed to suck at this."

Anytime you start heaping shame and despair on yourself, step back and remember that you are still learning. Yes, you're not where you want to be, but you are on your way.

After you've put in ten years of consistent work, you can reevaluate if you really do suck at it.

TOOL NUMBER 14

REMEMBER THAT EVERYONE IS LYING TO YOU

Another mantra to remember anytime you hear the crazy success stories is, "There is always a dark side." There is always a long path of failed experiments.

Yes, learn from the success of others, but don't take it as a judgment on your current path.

TOOL NUMBER 15

TREAT EVERYTHING AS AN EXPERIMENT

"Failure is an event, not a person." —Zig Ziglar

Treat all of your work as a series of experiments. You are doing the best you can with the current knowledge that you have. At the end of this, you will have more knowledge for the next experiment.

Here are the steps:

1. Make observations
2. Form a hypothesis
3. Make a prediction
4. Perform an experiment
5. Analyze the results of the experiment
6. Draw a conclusion
7. Report your results
8. Go back to step 1

TOOL NUMBER 16

BUILD A BOARD OF DIRECTORS

This book took me two years to write. I rewrote the entire

manuscript from scratch three different times. All of this was driven by a handful of people who read what I had written and told me it wasn't good enough yet.

You need a small group of people—two to five—who will both hold your feet to the fire when you want to settle for less than your best and will tell you that it's time to release your work into the world when you're spinning in fear and perfectionism.

TOOL NUMBER 17
FIND AND FOLLOW THE RIGHT MENTOR

Most people suck at most things, me included. I am really good at one or two things, but you should ignore my advice on most everything else.

This is true for all people.

Just because someone is a great speaker doesn't make them a great mother or father. Just because someone has built a successful business doesn't mean they know how to properly manage people.

First, identify the problem you need advice on.

What is the current roadblock to your career that you could use some help on? Where are you stuck and feel like you're making no progress?

You have to have a specific problem you're dealing with before you try to find help.

Second, identify three potential mentors.

I am a strong advocate against trying to find a "life coach" or a mentor who will give you advice on lots of areas of your life and business. Most people are good at only a few things, but they will give you advice on anything you ask.

People who are brilliant painters but never sold a painting will still give you advice on finding patrons if you ask. People who are brilliant businessmen but have a horrible home life will still give you marriage advice if you ask.

It is important to find people you believe have solved the particular problem you are currently dealing with. If you are struggling to find an audience for your photography, find three people who have solved this problem. If you are struggling to find an agent for your novel, find three authors who have successfully and recently found an agent.

For most of these things, if you are paying attention to your field, you probably already can identify three potential mentors. If not, do your research. Look up popular websites and online radio shows in your field. Ask friends in your field who they read and listen to.

Your goal is to find three people who have solved the problem you are currently dealing with and are somewhat likely to respond. Don't reach out to the top A-listers in your industry. If you try to get ahold of the person who won three Grammys last year, you probably won't get through.

I recommend starting with mentors who are slightly ahead of you. Find people who are where you would like to be in the next two to three years. They don't have to be huge, world-renowned successes. They just need to be people who are successfully overcoming your current roadblocks.

Third, consume everything those people have ever created.

Read every article you can find. Listen to every interview they've done. Watch every presentation they've given. Read their books.

This step is the most important, and the one people often skip.

First off, you may find the answer to your question. If you are stuck on trying to find an audience for your music, you may find an interview with your favorite musician where she gives step-by-step instructions on how she did it. You can stop on this step and go solve your problem.

Second, it is important to invest your own time before you ask the potential mentor to invest their time.

I often have people asking me questions that I have answered for free on my website multiple times. It shows they did not do their research.

They don't want to invest their own time in consuming what I have already put out for free. They would rather take the shortcut and ask me to, instead, invest some of my time.

Take the time to consume everything the potential mentor has put out into the world. You'll learn a ton and be set up for success in the next steps.

Fourth, ask a short, specific question.

Please do not send a huge backstory of what's gone wrong and then ask a question like "What should I do now?"

A big, ambiguous question like that would take a lot of back-and-forth emailing to sift through it all.

When you reach out to someone who is an established authority or success story in their field, ask just one or two specific questions that can be answered quickly and concisely.

Assume the person on the other end will only have two sentences to answer your question. What would you ask?

Remember that your goal is to have this person be your mentor for an extended period of time. Your goal is not to get all their advice at once. Simply ask a question that they can quickly answer and tell you what to do next.

For instance, "I've tried A and B so far and read an article where you recommended C. I'm struggling with C because of D. What do you think I should try next?"

A question like that does several things. First, it shows you are trying things on your own. Second, it shows you've done your research. Third, it's something they can give advice on quickly.

Your goal with this is to simply get a response.

Side note: Many will not respond. That's why I recommend starting with three people who aren't huge celebrities in your field. Don't be discouraged if it takes some time to connect with people. Always assume the best about them. You will still learn so much during the process of consuming their content.

Fifth, take their advice and then report back.

People make two common mistakes when they receive advice from a mentor.

First, they argue. They say why that won't work for them or that they've already tried something like that.

Second, they ignore. They never actually do the advice they were given.

Please don't be that person.

Unless their advice is illegal, immoral, or physically dangerous, do what they say without question. Treat it as another experiment. Again, your goal isn't only to solve this particular problem, it's to find a long-term mentor.

People enjoy helping people who actually do things. If you immediately put their advice into practice and then report back to them the results, you will show you are worth their time in helping and are much more likely to continue getting their help.

Once you report back, ask a follow-up question that is still short and specific.

Sixth, maintain ongoing, respectful contact.

At this point, you should have a rapport with the person. Follow up, but only as needed. I have a mentor I speak with on a weekly basis. I also have a mentor I reach out to, at most twice a year, and we usually speak for less than an hour.

You have to use your own judgement on how often to seek the person's advice, but it depends on your project and the mentor's willingness to give you their time.

The win is to have a person who is an expert in a particular field who you can call on when you need help in that area. I have a half a dozen different people I am connected to that I know I can reach out to if I need their help.

TOOL NUMBER 18
GET A THERAPIST

Don't skip over this one.

If one practice has most impacted my personal and professional life, it's seeing a therapist on a regular basis. I see mine every week. In the last two years since I've been seeing my current therapist, I've had exactly one week when I didn't have something I needed to work through with him.

There are two important sides to seeing a therapist.

First, of course, you want a good therapist. You want someone who will listen, not try to fix you, and mostly be a sounding board who helps you find yourself.

Second, and most importantly, it forces you to stop your crazy pace of life, sit down, and deal with your shit.

Yes, it's expensive. Yes, it's annoying. Yes, it's embarrassing. And yes, it's worth it.

TOOL NUMBER 19
ALWAYS ASK WHY

Always question everything. Why are you doing what you're doing? Why are things the way they are? Why do people do it this way? Why do I feel this way? Why do I believe this?

TOOL NUMBER 20
TRUST YOURSELF

You are the golden Buddha.

When you do things that are healthy and good, that is you. When you do things that are unhealthy and bad, that's just the layers on top. It's not you.

Hold on to that. Trust yourself. You'll find your way.

ACKNOWLEDGMENTS

Candace, you're the obvious hero of this story. While I was writing this book we celebrated our fifteen-year marriage anniversary. If you count the years we dated, we've been together over half our lives. In all that time you never once questioned my ability to run down my dream. You let me flail and fail and find my way. I saw several other men whose wives gave them hell for their dreams and you never once did that. You're the strongest person I know. I love you more than anything and still wonder how I got such an amazing woman to throw in with me. As Zig said on those recordings all those years ago..."If you leave me, I'm going with you."

Conner and Maxwell, you were too little to remember most of this story, but you often got the raw end of the deal. My hope is that the man I've become through this process is someone you can be proud of and learn from. I love you both more than anything and thank you for constantly showing me that we all have that perfect light inside of us.

Mom and Dad, you always assumed I could accomplish whatever I set out to do. My courage often came from knowing both that you would love me and support me no matter what I went after, and that you would be there to help if I got myself into a tough spot. I love you both and am so thankful to have you in my life.

Shawn Coyne, my editor, business partner, and friend. I kept wanting to settle for a book that wasn't my best, and you wouldn't let me. You brought me to the end of myself so I could finally find this book and do the best writing I've ever done. I'm eternally grateful for all you've poured into me over the last three years.

Josh Kaufman, you pulled me from the pit of despair more times than I can count. When you stopped business coaching and fired me as a client, I said, "You know, this just means you're going to keep coaching me for free." You replied, "I'm okay with that." And so you were. Thank you for being the wise, kind friend that is always willing to listen, encourage, and help.

To all the authors who hired me over the years, thanks for working with me and teaching me. Particularly Daniel Pink, Dan Heath, Pamela Slim, Hugh MacLeod, Hugh Howey, Barbara Corcoran, Ramit Sethi, and Dan Ariely were those early clients who helped me get a start in the industry.

Daniel Pink, not long after we were working together we met for the first time in person over lunch. It was during a particularly low point in my journey. I shared a little bit with you. You encouraged me and then sort of chuckled and said, "Tim, you're doing fine. You're going to be great." There were a lot of times when I thought about that moment and it gave me the encouragement to keep going.

Steven Pressfield, thank you for writing *The War of Art* and so many other amazing books that line my book shelves. Your work gave me permission to keep running down my dreams when everything around me told me it was time to quit. Not to mention, a five-minute conversation with you fixed a problem in this book I had been churning on for six months.

Todd Sattersten, Jill Murphy, Colleen Wainwright, Gene Kim, Dan Portnoy, Mark Fesmire, Jeff Goins, Ryan Holiday...I know I'm forgetting people...you have each been my muses and encouragement and members of my board of directors. Some of you are in this book by name and others are in it by what I've learned.

They say it takes a village, and I've had the best of the best.

H. 11/18

14776729R00139

Made in the USA
Lexington, KY
09 November 2018